Event Evaluation:

Theory and Methods for Event Management and Tourism

Donald Getz, PhD.

Goodfellow Publishers Ltd

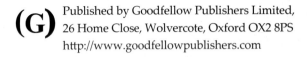

Published by Goodfellow Publishers Limited,
26 Home Close, Wolvercote, Oxford OX2 8PS
http://www.goodfellowpublishers.com

British Library Cataloguing in Publication Data: a catalogue
record for this title is available from the British Library.

Library of Congress Catalog Card Number: on file.

ISBN: 978-1-9113-9665-9

The Events Management Theory and Methods Series

Copyright © Donald Getz, 2018

Design and typesetting by P.K. McBride, www.macbride.org.uk

Cover design by Cylinder

Printed by Marston Book Services, www.marston.co.uk

Contents

List of Figures

Introduction to the Events Management Theory and Methods Series

Event management as a field of study and professional practice has its textbooks with plenty of models and advice, a body of knowledge (EMBOK), competency standards (MBECS) and professional associations with their codes of conduct. But to what extent is it truly an applied management field? In other words, where is the management theory in event management, how is it being used, and what are the practical applications?

Event tourism is a related field, one that is defined by the roles events play in tourism and economic development. The primary consideration has always been economic, although increasingly events and managed event portfolios meet more diverse goals for cities and countries. While the economic aspects have been well developed, especially economic impact assessment and forecasting, the application of management theory to event tourism has not received adequate attention.

In this book series we launch a process of examining the extent to which mainstream theory is being employed to develop event-specific theory, and to influence the practice of event management and event tourism. This is a very big task, as there are numerous possible theories, models and concepts, and virtually unlimited advice available on the management of firms, small and family businesses, government agencies and not-for-profits. Inevitably, we will have to be selective.

The starting point is theory. Scientific theory must both explain a phenomenon, and be able to predict what will happen. Experiments are the dominant form of classical theory development. But for management, predictive capabilities are usually lacking; it might be wiser to speak of theory in development, or theory fragments. It is often the process of theory development that marks research in management, including the testing of hypotheses and the formulation of propositions. Models, frameworks, concepts and sets of propositions are all part of this development.

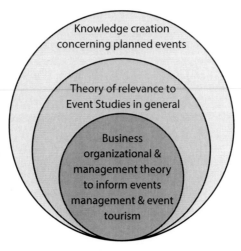

The diagram illustrates this approach. All knowledge creation has potential application to management, as does theory from any discipline or field. The critical factor for this series is how the theory and related methods can be applied. In the core of this diagram are management and business theories which are the most directly pertinent, and they are often derived from foundation disciplines.

All the books in this series will be relatively short, and similarly structured. They are designed to be used by teachers who need theoretical foundations and case studies for their classes, by students in need of reference works, by professionals wanting increased understanding alongside practical methods, and by agencies or associations that want their members and stakeholders to have access to a library of valuable resources. The nature of the series is that as it grows, components can be assembled by request. That is, users can order a book or collection of chapters to exactly suit their needs.

All the books will introduce the theory, show how it is being used in the events sector through a literature review, incorporate examples and case studies written by researchers and/or practitioners, and contain methods that can be used effectively in the real world. Online resources will include annotated bibliographies, additional resources, and for teachers an instructor's manual and set of power-point slides.

Preface To Event Evaluation

Key objectives of the book:

1 Inform readers on evaluation theory and methods for events and event tourism, including key concepts and definitions.
2 Discuss key evaluation challenges for events and event tourism.
3 Provide a comprehensive evaluation system that can be fully integrated into event and tourism organisations.
4 Develop professionalism for evaluators in these fields.
5 Recommend the goals, key performance indicators and methods for evaluation.
6 Connect readers to the research literature pertinent to evaluation.

Event and tourism organisations and event managers need to implement a continuous process of evaluation in order to become learning organisations, to achieve their goals, and to meet all standards that are applicable. Some funding bodies insist that event organisers meet performance standards in order to qualify, while others demand comprehensive evaluations and public accountability. In these environments, a comprehensive evaluation system becomes essential, as does professionalism by evaluators.

Most evaluation at the level of a single event is related to problem solving and support for decision making, and these require fairly straightforward data collection techniques. More complex policy and programme evaluations that require determination or evidence of goal attainment can be approached through theory-based evaluations or logic models, and these are covered in this book. The biggest challenge of all is to determine the worth or value of an event, programme or policy, and a great deal of advice is provided on that challenging task, with emphasis on clarifying various perspectives on value.

In this book impacts and impact assessment are introduced, but a separate impact assessment book will provide details on methods for measuring and evaluating social, cultural, ecological, and economic impacts of events, as well as those relating to the built environment. That is where most of the tourism issues arise.

What this book is not

This book is not about research methods, it only introduces the methods and measures needed by evaluators; statistics are completely avoided. Evaluation has to be based on good research much of the time, so the evaluator's skills have to include research methods. On the other hand, people and organisations evaluate qualitatively all the time, in making judgements, giving advice on how things can be improved, and basing decisions on available information. Many events and programmes are valued intrinsically, based on cultural and personal values, for which research and metrics are not necessarily wanted or required.

The simple techniques explained in this book, such as checklists and systematic observation, can be used by any evaluator, but the more complex ones require a foundation in research methods. Several books are available specific to tourism, sport, leisure and events.

Some relevant books on research and methods

Getz, D. and Page, S. (2016). *Tourism Studies* (3d.ed). London: Routledge.

Getz, D. (2013) *Event Tourism*. NY Cognizant.

Long, J. (2007). *Researching Leisure, Sport and Tourism* (2d ed). Sage.

Richards, G., & Munsters, W. (2010). *Cultural Tourism Research Methods*. Wallingford, UK: CABI.

Smith, S. (2010). *Practical Tourism Research*. Wallingford, UK: CABI.

Veal, A.J. (2017). *Research Methods for Leisure and Tourism*. Pearson.

Aknowledgements

Books do not get written on a blank slate, there are always those whose important contributions must be acknowledged. First, special thanks go to two contributors of case studies: Colin Beard (Sheffield-Hallam University) and Richard Shipway (Bournemouth University). Critical parts of this book have their origins in work related to development of the Event Compass, a project that occurred under the auspices of Mid Sweden University in Ostersund, with Robert Pettersson as team leader. Myself and Steve Brown from South Australia have acted as advisors, and we all contributed to the published article on evaluation that is cited herein.

Some ideas and material are based on a major, two-year research and development project funded by BFUF – the research and development foundation of the Swedish Hospitality and Tourism Industry. The project was directed by and for RF, the Swedish Sport Confederation, to improve competency, sustainability and competitiveness in the sport events sector. However, the recommendations arising from this project, in the form of guidelines, can be applied to all events and event tourism situations.

My previous books have provided inspiration and material, all the way back to the first one entitled *Festivals, Special Events and Tourism* (1991). *Event Studies* (third edition, co-authored with Stephen Page in 2016), *Event Management and Event Tourism* (Cognizant, 2005) and *Event Tourism* (Cognizant, 2013) provide a considerable amount of background and elaboration.

1 Basic Concepts and Definitions

Learning objectives

- ☐ Learn why evaluation is essential in professional practice.
- ☐ Understand why impact assessment is not necessarily evaluation and why impacts do not equate with benefits.
- ☐ Understand how evaluation for events and event tourism is unique.
- ☐ Appreciate how different types of events pose unique evaluation challenges.
- ☐ Be able to conduct evaluations that implement the event body of knowledge (EMBOK), meeting and business events competency standards (MBECS) and other pertinent standards.
- ☐ Know the standards for professional evaluators and competent evaluations.

1.1 Introduction

To start thinking about evaluation of events and event tourism, consider these four challenging scenarios:

1 An event manager wants to obtain certification as a sustainable event, but the cost and necessity of doing so is in doubt. The event has data on its energy, water and waste processes, but what other information is needed? What specific evidence will be sufficient to help make the right decision? What arguments can be used?

2 Customers at a festival are unhappy, year after year attendance is dropping, and the financial viability of the event is threatened. The owners ask an evaluation professional to help determine the causes and recommend solutions. How should this evaluation project be designed to help save the event?

3 A corporation wants to create an event to enhance its brand and develop a community of loyal customers. How exactly should evaluation be built into the design, organisation and operations of this new event?

4 Local governments assist events in many ways, often including a partnership with tourism and hospitality agencies to bid on sport events and conventions, and thereby generate tourism impact. They also seek to foster social integration and boost culture through programmes of festivals and celebrations. In

creating and managing these 'portfolios' of events, serving many different interest groups with sometimes complimentary and sometimes conflicting goals, how do governments determine which events or types of event best meet their goals? What is each event worth?

Scenario 1 suggests the need for a monitoring system to inform strategy and decisions on going green, being sustainable and getting certified. Monitoring and data collection are essential for planning and decision-making, and knowing what data to collect and how to analyse data to facilitate decision-making are evaluation skills. As to the nature of evidence and how to make arguments, the professional evaluator must combine technical skills with knowledge of how decisions are made.

Scenario 2 describes the context for many event evaluation projects – to identify and solve problems. Sometimes the evaluation is done internally, or by consultants and external stakeholders. If the event in the scenario has sponsors, they might very well want to abandon the festival, or perhaps they will insist on an impartial evaluation with the hope of getting it back on a successful track. Determining the cause of a problem is one thing, but making recommendations to the owners for a solution requires an even higher level of problem-solving.

Scenario 3 gets to the necessity of building evaluation into events right from the beginning, with data collection, monitoring, analysis and decision-support being fully integrated in design and all management functions. The evaluator has models for this kind of system, and knows how to implement evaluation to ensure success.

Scenario 4 deals with event portfolios, tourism, and complex evaluations that examine impacts and the effectiveness of strategies. This type of evaluation gets to the heart of 'why and how' events are valued. How do different stakeholders value events, and how can anyone answer the question "what is an event worth"?

By the end of the book readers should be able to answer the questions posed in these scenarios – they represent the essence of event and event-tourism evaluation.

Evaluation is an essential management function of information gathering and feedback through which processes can be improved, goals more effectively attained, and by which organisations can learn and adapt. To 'evaluate' is also to place a value on something, or to pass judgment on its quality, effectiveness or worth. Evaluation occurs within policy, planning and decision-making processes and is therefore often political in nature.

Evaluation is *applied*, meaning it always has a purpose. The research done to develop theory is not evaluation, but theory can be important to the evaluation process. When students learn research methods and statistics they are not learning how to do evaluation, but are mastering tools that can be used by evaluators.

Despite recognition of evaluation's vital role in policy making, managerial improvement and event design, it has been a minor theme in the literature on planned events. Clifton et al. (2012: 89), following an evaluation of festivals in the UK, argued that "in a culture of evidence-based decision-making, reliable, and robust evaluation is also essential." Their review concluded that serious weaknesses occurred in the context of evaluating public policy initiatives related to events: a lack of prioritization, advocacy presented as evaluation, and poor quality reporting; complex and politically sensitive objectives are difficult to objectify, while evaluation itself has been under-resourced or viewed as optional.

Impact assessment is a special case of evaluation. When events or programmes are designed to achieve certain outcomes (or impacts), a goal-attainment evaluation is required. The impact assessment might become part of determining the worth of the event or programme, alongside other considerations such as cost-benefit evaluation, opportunity costs and alternatives, and stakeholder opinions. Economic impact assessment has dominated the tourism literature, but there is evident a paradigm shift towards taking a longer-term perspective on the value of events and their legacies within a triple-bottom-line framework. This concern is now expanding to consider managed portfolios and entire populations of events, which compounds the evaluator's challenges. In this book the discussion of impact assessment is commenced, but a separate book will be devoted to the many complex theories and issues involved.

Evaluation of organisations, personnel and event quality, and event experiences is a key issue in the planned-events sector. It is of critical importance to ensure success from the multiple perspectives of owners, producers, customers, and other stakeholders. Increasingly, evaluation is tied to certification, which is in itself required by many funding agencies and by those granting rights to bid on and produce events. Evaluation is at the heart of sustainability, as without it organisations cannot learn and improve nor can they be held accountable for costs and benefits.

Event evaluation continues to evolve, expand, and become more complex as the discourse on events and event tourism evolves. The basic applications remain intact, including placing a value on events and their sub-elements through visitor satisfaction or return on investment (ROI) measures, and the usual methods remain important, such as visitor satisfaction or economic impact assessment. But event evaluation must now meet much broader objectives including sustainability (in itself a complex matter), encompassing questions of social responsibility, cultural and environmental costs and benefits.

1.2 Unique aspects of planned events and event tourism

Planned events are all different, with unique evaluation questions and practical challenges. In Chapter 13 evaluation issues and methods related to the main types of events are examined, but in this introductory chapter some fundamentals are presented. A complete discussion can be found in the book *Event Studies* (third edition by Getz and Page, 2016).

Much of the generic literature on evaluation concerns policies and programmes – particularly in the health and education fields. The dominant purpose of these evaluations is determining what works and how, proving cause and effect, and drawing conclusions about the merit and worth of interventions. Programmes are generally implemented by one agency with a specific mandate (such as leisure or education or social welfare) whereas events have so many stakeholders that complexity is the norm, even ambiguity about who is attempting to achieve what. Programmes often seek to demonstrate cause and effect in justifying their existence, whereas events can simply happen. Private event owners might want a good return on their investment and effort, but many producers believe in the intrinsic worth of events, with no need for 'proof' of benefits. Other stakeholders, such as grant givers or sponsors, might be content in knowing that people enjoyed the event. But when programmes and events are set up to cause change within a policy field, they become instruments and their outputs and impacts must be evaluated.

The majority of event evaluation is done to support decisions and solve problems, and only rarely is it to determine the overall worth of the event to society or particular stakeholders. Evaluating long-term impacts is not a primary consideration in event management, but does hold higher priority when tourism and economic development are factors.

The core of Event Studies is the experience and meanings attached to it, and experiences are a co-creation of producers and attendees. The nature and quality of the experience are of concern to evaluators. In addition, there are almost always constraints involved in getting events produced on time, within budget, and to a high standard of service and programme quality – with only one brief period to get it right.

1.2.1 Event tourism

Using events as an instrument of tourism, economic development and place marketing is very common, and it helps explain why there are so many, and why they figure so prominently in city and country policies and strategies. When tourism and development are part of the equation, and especially when they are the main feature of events (e.g., when they are bid on and won competitively) the emphasis and methods of evaluation change. In this context there will always be forecasts of costs and benefits (and all too often the imputed benefits are deliberately exaggerated and the costs downplayed), followed by some accounting of tourism impacts – that is, how many tourists were attracted and how much did they spend, what was the media impact, and did the destination/city gain in terms of image, new infrastructure, etc.? The evaluator will be faced with an enormous challenge – to compile and assess *all* costs and benefits, including their distribution (some people win, others pay) and to ensure a fair and open accounting.

The *legacy* will also be of primary concern, meaning the long-term changes that an event or events within a managed portfolio can provide, such as new venues and the future events they facilitate, structural shifts in the economy to make it more competitive, or enhanced self-reliance. These imputed legacy impacts are difficult to prove, are often controversial, and are increasingly a mix of economic, social, cultural and environmental outcomes – making for a highly complex evaluation.

The most common forms of evaluation within event tourism will be forecasts (were they accurate?), measures of marketing effectiveness, financial assessments (profit and loss, debt), visitor studies (including motivation, satisfaction and spending) and economic impact assessments. Comprehensive cost-benefit evaluations are rare, but this author thinks they should be required by law for all major investments. Distributional effects and externalities (such as pollution, amenity loss, social displacement) are seldom taken into account, but they should be.

1.2.3 Value perspectives

Figure 1.1 (overleaf) is the first of a series summarizing value perspectives, as discussed fully in Chapter 2. These reflect the interests of different stakeholder groups, although overlapping interests is normal. The book *The Value of Events* (Lundberg et al., 2017) is one foundation for this series.

1.3 Professional practice

Evaluation is so essential that all professionals require pertinent knowledge, but specialist skills in this area should be provided through certification offered by institutions and/or associations. It is not well developed in the literature, unfortunately.

Goldblatt's text *Special Events* (6th ed., 2011:65) explains that evaluation is a dynamic process, should include stakeholder input, and is connected to setting Key Performance Indicators (KPIs) for the event. Allen et al. (2011:292) stated: "… event evaluation is critical to the event management process. It is the final step in the planning process, where the goals and objectives set at the start of an event are used as benchmarks to determine its final outcomes and success." Allen et al. also said that the triple-bottom-line approach is increasingly recognized by governments and researchers alike. Their textbook, *Festival and Special Event Management* contains a full description of the evaluation process from this perspective, including instructive case studies.

Research on the evaluation practices of event managers, or of development and tourism agencies have been infrequent, consequently we have an incomplete and perhaps dated picture of the state-of-art. Carlsen et al. (2000) surveyed the literature on evaluation and impact assessment and reported on a Delphi survey of event experts in Australia that revealed the most important perceived pre and post-event evaluation topics and measures. While a standardized approach was desired, that aim has never been achieved. Wood (2009a: 175) concluded from

Figure 1.1: Value perspectives and major evaluation challenges

Value perspective	Major evaluation challenges
Economic value: According to Dwyer et al. (2010: 1) tourism makes an 'economic contribution' to several key variables: gross domestic (or regional) product; household income; value added, foreign exchange earnings and employment. "Tourism's total economic contribution (both direct and indirect) measures the size and overall significance of the tourism industry within an economy". 'Economic impact', on the other hand, refers to changes caused by specific events or activities as 'shocks' to the system. ■ Events can serve as catalysts for infrastructure development (e.g., roads, mass transit) and increased capacity to attract future events and tourists through new venues and heightened image, or through improved organisation and marketing of the destination (Getz, 2013).	■ Events and tourism can be a factor in economic development and growth for business, cities, regions and countries, but do the costs always justify the benefits? Opportunity costs are seldom considered (i.e. alternative ways to attain goals or other uses of resources). ■ The distributional effects (i.e., who pays and who gains) and externalities (like carbon pollution) are often ignored. ■ Imputed economic benefits are often used to justify political decisions, and multipliers or other econometric models are often used to deliberately exaggerate imputed benefits. ■ Triple-bottom-line and sustainability thinking is replacing a narrow focus on economics, raising the need for either uniform metrics or cost/benefit assessments that balance tangibles and intangibles.
Tourism value: Specific tourism roles played by events (from Getz, 2013) include: attraction, animator catalyst, image making and place marketing. Image enhancements and improved competitive positioning can also be considered as tourism value linked to events.	Not all events generate positive economic or tourism value – to do so they have to attract tourists who would not otherwise travel to the destination, and their spending ('new money') has to exceed costs.
Financial value: this is a sub-set of economic value and business value, specifically the profit and loss accruing to event organisations or tourist organisations. ■ Can include money raised for charity. 'Profit', or surplus revenue, is necessary for ALL events – if only to ensure there is money in the bank, a reserve fund, to cover various contingencies.	■ Detailed and certified accounts are needed ■ There could be difficulty in measuring profit/surplus and loss for institutions and charities that do not specifically pursue profit but depend upon grants and sponsorship

UK studies that festivals were marked by "…ill-thought-out objectives, which are then not assessed, leaving evaluation to the basics of attendance counts, questionable economic impact measures, and assessment of the functional aspects of the event (Pugh & Wood, 2004; Thomas & Wood, 2003)." "In the UK, … many departments did not undertake any type of evaluation and those that did focused on attendance figures, participant feedback, and attendee satisfaction (Thomas & Wood, 2003)."

O'Sullivan et al. (2009) reviewed event evaluations by local governments in Wales and concluded that most had focused on improving processes and measuring economic impacts; social-cultural objectives were common, but these outcomes were not usually evaluated. Looking back, Wood (2017:31) concluded in the UK there is still "a need for greater evidence to prove value and justify expenditure…", but there are fewer resources to do the necessary evaluation.

Williams and Bowdin (2007) reviewed event evaluation literature and studied seven UK arts festivals as to their evaluation purposes, methods and uses. They concluded that evaluation was well understood in terms of its roles in measuring event success related to goals, shaping the planning process, meeting stakeholder expectations, and making improvements. The methods, data and objects of the arts festivals' evaluations were summarized, noting that the audience in particular was of extreme importance, as well as financial performance, media coverage, artists and other stakeholders. Robertson et al. (2009) found that 47 of 56 festival directors from a UK sample did a formal evaluation of their event, of which 77% measured community involvement or community satisfaction levels; 60% said they gained feedback from sponsors and 53% undertook an economic impact evaluation. Interestingly, they discovered that older festivals were less likely to evaluate community involvement or satisfaction or performer satisfaction.

Figure 1.2: Value perspectives and challenges (continued)

Value perspective	Major evaluation challenges
Built environment value: the contribution of events and tourism to form, functioning and livability of communities and cities, linked to animation of spaces, leisure opportunities, design, heritage conservation.	The meaning of 'livability' could vary a lot. Establishing links between events/tourism and enhanced livability could be difficult. ▪ 'Heritage' is a value-laden term so evaluators must consider different stakeholders and perspectives.
Ecological value could be measured by direct contributions to conservation, habitat rehabilitation, or carbon offsetting. Events pursuing green and sustainability strategies are explicitly trying to create ecological value. Education for environmentalism can be part of an event's transforming processes.	▪ Ecological footprint calculation is complex, and models have to be customized to particular countries or regions (see Collins and Cooper, 2017; Andersson et al., 2013) ▪ Evaluators have a difficult task to measure learning, attitudinal and behavioural changes related to ecological value production
Heritage value: events and tourism can contribute to the appreciation and preservation of heritage, whether tangible (e.g. buildings, costumes, recipes) or intangible (e.g., rituals, symbols). This could also be linked to measures of civic or national pride. The interpretation of historical events and traditions can give rise to considerable conflict of values.	▪ Heritage is often contested, with disagreements about accuracy or whose perspective is dominant (i.e., as expressions of power) ▪ Civic pride has been investigated by Wood (2006)

The literature on event and tourism impact assessment is much more fully developed, but it reflects a bias towards the demonstration of purported economic benefits in support of development and investment. A consortium of UK sponsors has created a website full of impact assessment advice and examples called EventImpacts (www.eventimpacts.com). Its contents cover attendance, economic, social, environmental and media impacts.

1.3.1 Evaluation in EMBOK and MBECS

EMBOK, the event management body of knowledge, does not explicitly recognize or discuss evaluation. Presumably it is a skill or technique needed to realize the core values and perform the main management functions, as implied in this quote from Silvers et al. (2005:194) "The core values of creativity, strategic thinking, continuous improvement, ethics, and integration are the values that must permeate all decisions throughout event management regarding every element, phase, and process."

Within MBECS, meeting and business event competency standards (MPI, 2012) evaluation is an integral part of both strategic and project management. For example, under 'strategic planning' the following actions are specified:

1 *Manage Strategic Plan for Meeting or Event* (develop mission, goals, objectives: determine feasibility; determine requirements to carry out meeting/event; develop financial summary; monitor strategic plan);

2 *Develop Sustainability Plan for Meeting or Event* (implement plan; demonstrate environmental responsibility);

3 *Measure Value of Meetings and Business Events* (develop evaluation plan; measure return on investment; evaluate/audit; evaluate effectiveness of risk management plan).

Elsewhere more specific monitoring and evaluation actions are specified, such as 'evaluate staff'.

1.3.2 Professional event evaluator

Stufflebeam and Coryn (2014) consider evaluators to be professionals, and there exist a number of professional associations such as the American Evaluation Association (AEA) that should be consulted for anyone interested in this line of work. Event and tourism evaluation is a sub-set of the generic field. AEA has formulated principles for evaluators, and the main headings are reproduced below. Evaluators should become familiar with all these principles and sub-points, so follow this source:

The Principles (http://www.eval.org/p/cm/ld/fid=51)

A *Systematic Inquiry*: Evaluators conduct systematic, data-based inquiries.

B *Competence*: Evaluators provide competent performance to stakeholders.

C *Integrity/Honesty*: Evaluators display honesty and integrity in their own behaviour, and attempt to ensure the honesty and integrity of the entire evaluation process.

D *Respect for People*: Evaluators respect the security, dignity and self-worth of respondents, programme participants, clients, and other evaluation stakeholders.

E *Responsibilities for General and Public Welfare*: Evaluators articulate and take into account the diversity of general and public interests and values that may be related to the evaluation.

What would be the tasks and qualifications for a 'Professional Event Evaluator'? Those who do evaluations will likely have direct experience with events, others will come from related occupations where evaluation is well developed. But do they have all the theory and technical skills needed? Stufflebeam and Coryn (2014:15) specified "Key areas of required expertise are research design, sampling, measurement, interviewing, observation, site visits, archival studies, case studies, focus groups, photography, database development and management, statistics, content analysis, cost analysis, policy analysis, synthesis, and computer technology." These skills have to be augmented by the ability to work with clients and stakeholders, write good reports, make presentations, and exercise wise judgment.

Figure 1.3: Value perspectives and challenges (continued)

Value perspective	Major evaluation challenges
Political value: Events have often been used as political tools. They can carry messages that are in fact propaganda, such as to reinforce an ideology, and they can attract attention to political figures who want to bask in the glory or spectacle surrounding events.	Evaluation of policies and events often touches upon ideology and partisan politics, possibly leading to conflicts and impaired utilization of results. Elite groups in society often back events for their own purposes, and that is a big equity issue.
Social value: These are benefits of events and tourism to society as a whole, or to defined social groups such as the economically disadvantaged ■ 'Social capital' is both an input and possible outcome, related to the establishment of networks, creating trust and collaboration. ■ 'Social marketing' is the aim of some events, being the creation of social value by informing and educating people about a cause and seeking to change attitudes and behaviour. ■ The 'inspirational effects' of sport events on society (do they inspire higher levels of activity and improve overall health?) have been examined (e.g., Ramchandani et al., 2017). ■ Legitimation of groups or sub-cultures through events is a theme.	Both attitudinal and behavioural changes / benefits attributable to events and tourism are difficult to prove, with plenty of mixed evidence. ■ It cannot be expected that one event will generate a profound or lasting change in society. ■ Events can become points of conflict when social and cultural values clash.

A curriculum in event evaluation would ideally begin with the same courses taken by event management and tourism students leading to a degree, followed by (or possibly taken in a parallel track) the evaluator specialization. If one does not understand the nature of events, event tourism and event management it will be difficult to do a credible evaluation. Mastering various research methods is a must.

1.3.3 Standards for professional evaluations

Stufflebeam and Coryn (2014) have also articulated the standards for a professional evaluation, and informed people should be able to tell a good one from something inadequate. I have summarized them here, and added some comments.

Utility standards

♦ Programme evaluations should serve the client's needs, and be of utility to them; other stakeholders might have a right to be consulted and obtain the results. This differentiates evaluation from pure research, but it raises some questions. What if the owners, funders or proponents of events and tourism do not want evaluation?!

♦ Stakeholder interests should be considered. In tourism and events that could mean every citizen! This standard is often ignored, but increasingly informed residents demand to be consulted and to hold events and tourism agencies accountable.

♦ Make values explicit. I think many funders of evaluations and impact assessments do not do this, but it is often clear that only economic impacts are being valued. There is increasing discourse, at least among academics, about the conflicting interests in society as reflected in events and tourism, such as who gains and who pays. Diverse values should be taken into account but often the values of various elite groups in society predominate.

Feasibility

♦ Evaluators will have to work with clients and stakeholders to determine a feasible study, within a given budget and timeframe. Experimental methods seldom work in events and tourism, but a variety of mixed methods are available to answer most questions – or at least to provide good evidence. Probably the most common issue in events and tourism is that reputable evaluations are not commissioned, followed closely by a failure to provide adequate resources. All too often money is lavished on feasibility studies and bids, then little or nothing follows the event. This lack of transparency, honesty and accountability has plagued the fields of event and tourism management for a long time.

♦ Use project management techniques (e.g., critical path).

♦ Efficiently use resources.

Propriety

♦ Evaluations should be conducted within legal and ethical bounds, taking into account the welfare of those who could be impacted.

♦ Respect stakeholder interests and human rights.

♦ Transparency and disclosure of findings.

Accuracy

♦ This refers to technical competence in performing evaluations, and reliability/validity of the information and analysis generated in evaluations.

♦ Methods have to be suitable to the purpose and context, yielding valid information and conclusions.

Accountability

♦ The evaluator should be accountable for the work, and be open to scrutiny.

♦ Full documentation is required. All too often event impact assessments are hidden.

♦ Evaluations should be amenable to meta-evaluations. This requires standardization of methods and measures.

Pseudo evaluation

Many evaluations and impact assessments do not meet professional standards, while others are deliberately unprofessional in their design. Stufflebeam and Coryn (2014) identified a number of 'pseudo-evaluations' that should raise red flags and be scrutinized carefully:

♦ Public relations (releasing positive data only about an event; exaggerating benefits, neglecting to include costs).

♦ Politically controlled (working for governments to serve their political purposes can also be called an exercise in propaganda – there have been far too many of these in the realm of events and tourism! Political motives infect many internal evaluations in institutions and corporations, such as when a manager wants to eliminate a programme or personnel).

♦ Pandering means giving the client exactly what they want, often a predetermined outcome, and this is unethical to say the least (let them do it themselves, evaluators should not get involved; an example is to demonstrate how an event generated a big ROI while deliberately ignoring costs and externalities).

♦ Evaluation by pretext occurs when evaluators are deliberately mislead as to the purpose or intended uses of their work (in other words, be careful of who you work for).

◆ Empowerment under the guise of evaluation: professional evaluators should not enable groups to make claims that they did an evaluation when in fact it was done by others; it is certainly useful to help events and agencies to do their own evaluations, but be cautious of playing political games.

◆ Selective release of customer data is not proper evaluation; for example, reporting only good feedback from event tourists and ignoring negatives. On open websites it is also disreputable to post false negative comments about competitors, but it is done.

'*Quasi-evaluations*' according to Stufflebeam and Coryn (2014) occur when the evaluation is designed to answer limited questions, such as 'did we meet our stated objectives?' as opposed to a full accounting of costs and benefits. Determining that an event met its objectives tells only part of the story when it comes to determining worth.

Figure 1.4: Value perspectives and challenges (continued)

Value perspective	Major evaluation challenges
Media value: this term could apply to the value media get from association with and coverage of events, or to the value to events of media coverage. ■ Events as image makers can contribute to positioning and attractiveness of cities and destinations.	■ Media value is sometimes quantified in monetary terms by reference to "advertising value equivalence" but it is a discredited method owing to its failure to account for actual impact.
Non-use values exist because many people see some cultural or public good in events, or in events and tourism in general (Andersson et al, 2017). ■ The *existence value* of an event can be measured by asking residents what they would pay to create or keep an event. ■ *Option value* indicates that people value having lots of choices. ■ *Bequest value* suggests that future generations should benefit, as in the maintenance of valued traditions.	Measuring non-use values requires surveys or direct questioning of people who do not attend; they can either be asked if they would pay or pay more to preserve an event that is threatened, to allocate more money from taxes to subsidize events, or in some way to support events they do not attend, then determining their reasons. ■ Non-use value dimensions might overlap, or be unclear to respondents. ■ Use and non-use values might be difficult to assess when events are free. ■ Some people will feel they suffer damages or psychic dis-benefits (e.g., stress) from events, and this has to be factored into the equation (if monetary values are attached, disbenefits have to be deducted from benefits).

Action research

This methodology transcends the various stages of evaluation described previously, in that the researcher/evaluator gets involved right at the beginning, helps shape the project/event, and participates in its evaluation and improvement. An internal staff person should be doing this as part of their job, but external evaluators can do the work, such as through partnership with a research institute. Ethical questions arise, particularly that of bias in determining the worth of the event as it continues to evolve. Action researchers cannot possibly remain completely objective, but if they are committed to honesty and thoroughness and improvement, that might be compensatory.

An 'actionable research' design was constructed by Peperkamp et al. (2015) to both evaluate festival experiences and contribute to event design. A research note on this work is included in Chapter 6.

Study questions

Each of the learning objectives suggests one or more study questions, as the reader should be able demonstrate the applicable knowledge drawing from this and subsequent chapters. Also useful are integrative study questions that could be answered in essays, as suggested below.

1   Discuss the nature and need for professionalism in event management and event-tourism evaluation, with reference to standards. Describe the knowledge and skills required.

2   Why is event and event-tourism evaluation unique? Discuss some unique challenges for a particular type of event. You will need Chapter 13 content for this problem.

Recommended additional readings and sources

American Evaluation Association (http://www.eval.org)

EventImpacts (www.eventimpacts.com).

EMBOK: Event Management Body of Knowledge (http://www.embok.org/index.php/embok-model)

Getz, D. (2013). *Event Tourism*. New York: Cognizant.

Getz, D., & Page, S. (2016). *Event Studies* (3d. ed.). London: Routledge.

MBECS: Meeting and Business Event Competency Standards Curriculum (https://www.mpiweb.org/docs/...and.../MBECS-Guide-APP-2-Standards.pdf)

Stufflebeam, S., & Coryn, C. (2014). *Evaluation Theory, Models, and Applications*, 2nd Edition. Jossey-Bass.

2 Value, Values and Evaluation

Learning objectives

☐ Be able to distinguish between 'value' and 'values', and learn how cultural and personal values affect evaluation.

☐ Learn the common meanings of 'evaluation' and the meaning of the following terms in the context of evaluation: worth, merit, probity, significance, feasibility, equity and safety .

☐ Be able to conduct evaluation that aims to solve problems, inform decisions, prove cause and effect, and establish the merit, worth and significance of events, policies, programmes and event tourism.

☐ Understand how intrinsic and extrinsic approaches affect evaluation.

☐ Understand the various justifications of public-sector intervention in events and tourism and how these generate evaluation questions, including: public good; social equity; market failure; economic efficiency; and sustainability.

☐ Appreciate that there are different perspectives on the value of events.

☐ Be able to define success and explain why evaluation is critical to success, however it is defined.

2.1 Introduction

Value, values, and evaluation: These terms hold different connotations and their proper usage is vital both in theory development and management. This chapter also discusses intrinsic and extrinsic approaches to valuing events, and looks closely at different ways in which events can be valued by stakeholders.

The published paper by Brown et al. (2015), illustrates the ways in which these terms are used, with event-related examples. *The Value of Events* (edited by Lundberg et al., 2017) provides an overview of concepts and definitions, contributed articles on different perspective on event and event-tourism value, and an ontological perspective on theory development.

2.2   Value and values

The noun and verb 'value' are commonly defined this way (drawing from multiple dictionaries):

♦ *Value* (noun): the regard that something is held to deserve; the importance, worth, or usefulness of something; the material or monetary worth of something

♦ *Value* (verb): to estimate the monetary worth of something or someone; to be important or beneficial; to hold a high opinion of something or someone

Note that 'value' or 'worth' is different from the values, beliefs or ideals held by people and groups.

♦ *Values* (noun): Important beliefs or ideals shared by individuals or cultural groups about what is good or bad, or has merit; principles or standards of behaviour; judgment as to what is important in life.

Values are generally based on religion, philosophical positions, and social norms; they have major influence on behavior and attitude and therefore influence politics and management. This is particularly true when a 'value set', such as those based on religion, culture, or perhaps social-economic status, influence's one's perception of an event's worth.

Figure 2.1: Value perspectives and challenges (continued)

Value perspective	Major evaluation challenges
Personal value Individuals can gain from attendance or other forms of involvement at events, such as volunteering, and this has been studied in the context of 'personal and social identity' formation and reinforcement, health, personal development or 'self actualisation', and hedonism – or just plain having fun. ■ 'Subjective well being' refers to a self-assessment of the effects arising from events or travel on happiness or satisfaction with life.	Theoretical foundations in social-psychology are required for meaningful evaluation of personal value. Established scales for involvement, serious leisure, wellbeing, and self development can be used.
Psychic value: This term is sometimes used to describe the benefits or value that people believe or perceive - whether true or not. They might include happiness, wellbeing, satisfaction, enjoyment, hedonism or fun. These are closely related to 'personal development'.	Evaluation of anything that occurs in the realms of perception and cognition requires theoretical foundation and special skill to ensure validity (that is, are you really measuring value?).
Family value: The family links personal with social value. Stadler and Jepson (2017) evaluated the effects of events on family socialization and 'quality of life'.	Members of families can hold different perspectives on value.

2.3 Evaluation

There are several widely recognized meanings of 'evaluation'. The first two are adapted from: *www.socialresearchmethods.net*, but altered to reflect events and event tourism contexts:

1 *Evaluation:* the assessment of the worth or merit of events or event tourism.

2 *Evaluation:* the technical process of obtaining information to learn, and to provide useful feedback about solving problems and improving management processes and event experiences.

Stufflebeam and Coryn (2014, 14) provided an operational definition:

3 "...*evaluation* is the systematic process of delineating, obtaining, reporting and applying descriptive and judgmental information about some object's merit, worth, probity, feasibility, safety, significance and/or equity."

Definition 1 stresses worth or merit, and these are defined below. Definition 2 stresses the decision-making and problem-solving roles of evaluation, these being the most common.

The third definition includes the main steps in evaluation, emphasizes that evaluation provides information and makes a judgment, and that it can be applied to a variety of end purposes.

♦ *Probity* in this context means integrity and being above reproach; it also covers legality and ethics.

♦ *Worth* and *merit* can be used synonymously, but some commentators make a distinction. Based on Scriven (1991a) in the *Evaluation Thesaurus*, consider these distinctions:

    • *Merit*: a subjective interpretation, as in an event deserving of support owing to its intrinsic value; merit can also mean the programme does what it is supposed to, or it meets its goals, without reference to context such as cost or political support.

    • *Worth* implies a quantitative and usually comparative measure of value, usually expressed in monetary terms. Context is always considered.

Consequently, in this language of evaluation, an event or programme can hold merit, but is not necessarily worth the price of admission or of being subsidized! Worth and merit entail different evaluation questions.

♦ *Significance* is also used in a specific way, referring to underlying values and meaning attached to evaluation. The significance of an event can be based on symbolic meaning, as in *iconic events* that represent the very best or toughest challenge to amateur athletes. Significance is not based on merit, so an iconic event might be a failure, or cost too much, or not be worth subsidizing by public authorities.

The Stufflebeam and Coryn (2014) definition of evaluation also refers to three more terms:

♦ *Feasibility* is a matter of cost and/or technical ability; the evaluation might consider if an event is possible, and affordable

♦ *Safety* refers to evaluations aimed at determining if something is safe.

♦ *Equity* in evaluation could refer to fairness, or determining the distribution of costs and benefits; e.g., do all people have access?

In Stufflebeam's CIPP evaluation model (in Kellaghan & Stufflebeam, 2003) there is another useful definition:

♦ "*Evaluation* is the process of delineating, obtaining and providing useful information for judging decision alternatives."

Again this is the definition focusing on decision support, but we need to define the key words:

♦ *Delineating*: determining what information is needed and how to get it.

♦ *Obtaining*: research and data collection; gathering evidence.

♦ *Providing*: putting the evidence into useful form and applying conclusions to the decision at hand.

♦ *Judging*: typical dictionary definitions make it clear that judgment is an essential part of evaluation:

    1 To give careful consideration before forming an opinion or estimation.

    2 To judge someone or something, as in picking the best apple pie.

According to Stufflebeam there are different kinds of decisions that evaluation contributes to. *Decisions* vary according to their importance (taking into account possible consequences and the amount of change being contemplated) and information availability (some decisions are supported by readily-available information, others require research) or theoretical guidance – do we know what we are doing or is it innovative and unpredictable?

2.4 Intrinsic versus extrinsic

Because people, social groups and political parties hold different values about life and government in general (often described in ideological terms like conservative versus liberal) it can be expected that events and event tourism are valued in quite different ways. To many people certain events are valued *intrinsically*, without reference to quantitative measures like money or development. For example, people value festivals as art forms or cultural expressions, and they do not need any justification for supporting them other than this acceptance of their intrinsic worth. Sport events can be valued this way, as many people believe sport to be good for social and health reasons.

But because events are often used as tools for policy and strategy, making them instruments of change, it is often desired to provide quantitative measures of their value or impact. This is evaluation by reference to *extrinsic* measures, and the most

Figure 2.2: Value perspectives and challenges (continued)

Value perspective	Major evaluation challenges
Utility; Use value *Use value*, or in economic terms utility, refers to the benefits people obtain directly by attending an event (see: Andersson et al., 2017, and Dwyer and Forsyth, 2017). For tourists this applies to the whole travel experience. Consumers exchange time, money, and effort for specific benefits derived from events and tourism; there are opportunity costs associated with every expenditure, that is, what else could be done to achieve similar or greater benefits?	Evaluators can use several approaches & methods, but considerable skill is required to obtain valid data and conduct appropriate analyses. ■ Use value can be equated with money spent, or several surrogate measures such as 'travel cost' which is a 'revealed preference' approach (Mortazavi and Heldt, 2017). ■ 'Stated preference' methods include 'consumer surplus' which can be measured through 'contingent valuation' by asking consumers about their 'willingness to pay' for an experience.
Consumer value The literature on consumer culture recognizes use value attached to a product, service, or experience plus exchange value (what is given up to consume), and value as perceived by consumers; in the event context this approach examines value co-creation (Goolaup and Mossberg, 2017). The existence of 'consumption communities' is relevant, and overlaps with 'social worlds' (Unruh, 1980) and 'special-interest tourism' such as *Foodies and Food Tourism* (Getz et al., 2014). *Iconic Events* (Getz, 2013) provide symbolic or semiotic value to these communities.	Consumer value is socially and culturally constructed (Goolaup and Mossberg, 2017), meaning it can vary substantially; evaluators must determine the meanings consumers and interest groups attach to event experiences.

common measure is money. This dichotomy of approaches to value – intrinsic versus extrinsic – can give rise to misunderstandings and conflicts. Indeed, some people in the arts and cultural communities resist quantitative measures of value, while others use economic impact assessments to strengthen the case for public support.

Andersson et al. (2012), adapting from McCarthy et al. (2004), created a matrix that distinguished between intrinsic and extrinsic value on the vertical axis and individual versus societal value on the horizontal. It has been reproduced in the book *The Value of Events* (Lundberg et al., 2017). The resulting categorization provides a framework for looking at stakeholders who evaluate events and the types of measures they use. Individuals may evaluate an event on the basis of their private needs, identity and experiences, while at the societal level health, welfare, cultural capital and social capital might be the main criteria employed by government agencies. This points to the need for a clearly defined subject of analysis meaning: from whose perspective is an analysis being made, i.e. is the focus of impacts on the individual, the company, the region, the state or the entire society?

Figure 2.3: Value perspectives and challenges (continued)

Value perspective	Major evaluation challenges
Community value: This category applies to residents of specific places, not communities of interest as in consumer value. 'Community development' or increased capacity to deal with their own problems is one possible outcome of collaborating to produce and host events. Environmental gains might be realized through venue development or urban renewal and design efforts, while livability might be enhanced through social integration and new leisure opportunities attributed to events and tourism. ■ Richards and Colombo (2017) emphasize 'network value' in discussing how events create value for cities through innovation, and this is part of the 'eventful cities' concept of Palmer and Richards (2010).	■ Communities are usually not homogeneous, so divergence of values is to be expected. ■ 'Livability' is a concept open to interpretation. ■ Communities must take ownership of events, at least in symbolic terms, in order to foster social capital and community development.
Cultural value: elements of language, religion customs, rituals, symbols and valued heritage that benefit from events and tourism. ■ Celebrating multiculturalism can bring people together. ■ 'Cultural capital'.	Benefits to the elements that define culture (e.g., values, language, religion, race, ethnicity); might include the concept of 'cultural capital'. ■ Events, especially the arts and cultural celebrations, are often valued intrinsically for their contribution to culture, preserving traditions, or bringing cultural groups together. ■ The very nature of celebration implies a sense of belonging. Rites and rituals also extend cultural value into religion and sometimes politics.

2.5 Justification for public-sector intervention

How do governments justify their involvement in events? Justification originates in policy fields as diverse as economic development and social welfare, urban and regional development or environmental sustainability. There are two sides to justification that relate to evaluation. The first comes from ideology, or the values governments place on events. The second relates to showing results, requiring formal audits and evaluations.

First and foremost is the *public good* argument, with government intervention justified on the basis that important benefits accrue to all residents, or the economy overall. Evaluators, in this context, sometimes have to demonstrate that the outcomes of events are *equitable* (i.e., not skewed towards one group, but that costs and benefits are equitably distributed). However, in some cases benefits are targeted towards one group, say the poor or children, and in these cases public good might be generated by solving important social problems. Such claims will be made within specific policy domains such as health or economic development, and the policies will seek substantial gains worth the investment. The justification will almost certainly reflect the ideology of government or dominant groups in society. Most importantly, there will be rules to follow in the use of resources and especially in terms of accountability.

Social equity is a principle that often arises when justifications are made for investing in events or venues, or social programmes in general. It is part of the public good discussion, with emphasis on providing equal access to important services and opportunities – including leisure, education, cultural expression, health and welfare.

Another justification, often made in conjunction with other public good claims, is *market failure*. This economic justification for public involvement rests on the premise that the 'free market' does not always provide sufficient incentive to stimulate entrepreneurial activity or investment. It is employed particularly with regard to investment in facilities and tourism marketing or economic development initiatives and might consist of subsidies, partnerships or incentives. It is possible to apply this argument to not-for-profit events, given that they provide public good that governments and industry are not meeting, such as festivals facilitating community development or multiculturalism. Evaluators might be asked to show a need, or a gap in services, or to demonstrate the critical importance of public intervention in securing desired results.

Less often employed as justification in the events and tourism realm is that governments can make money as entrepreneurs, especially to earn money to re-invest in important services or projects. *Economic efficiency* is a related argument, being the need for events to help pay for services and facilities that are intended to benefit residents.

Achieving *sustainability* goals might be a powerful justification. As discussed by Getz (2017) in an article in *Event Management*, events should make a positive contribution to the greening and sustainability policies of cities, from waste management to nature conservation, from reducing the ecological footprint to enhancing social integration and multi-cultural understanding.

Research note:

Getz, D. (2017). Developing a Framework for Sustainable Event Cities. *Event Management*, 21 (5), 575-591.

Abstract: This conceptual article considers meanings, and the process of attaining sustainability in eventful cities. New concepts and approaches are required to organise thoughts about, and set parameters for, discourse on sustainability in the realm of planned events. Ideas and recommendations contained in this article draw from a major research and development project in Sweden in which diverse stakeholders explicitly considered problems associated with event impact assessment and evaluation, and the roles of events in sustainable development.

Figure 2.4: Value perspectives and challenges (continued)

Value perspective	Major evaluation challenges
Brand value: brands can hold value for the owners when it comes to selling, and in terms of enhanced profitability arising from brand recognition and loyalty. ■ Events want their own brand to reflect their values, and if possible to engage in 'value-adding' activities for consumers to enhance profitability or satisfaction and loyalty. ■ 'Co-branding' with destinations has been discussed (Kaplanidou et al., 2012) and is particularly relevant to the concept of 'hallmark events' (Getz et al., 2012). Presumably co-branding adds value to both partners.	■ Mixed methods are likely necessary as brand value can be estimated in monetary terms when an event is sold, or by reference to what sponsors are willing to pay, or by subjectively by stakeholder perceptions ■ Co-branding value could be evaluated subjectively by examining visitor and non-visitor images, focusing on attributes (like events) that help generate interest or uniqueness
Business value: This is sub-set of economic value. Events and tourism can create benefits to individual businesses that arise from either a direct association with events or indirectly as a result of changes in economic activity by residents and tourists. ■ The term 'leveraging' is used to describe strategies for maximizing these benefits (Chalip, 2006) but is also applied to 'social leveraging'. ■ Prebensen (2017) suggests that additional business value accrues from networking and collaboration built around events and tourism. ■ Value to corporations might arise from CSR linked to events, such as providing volunteers and giving grants	■ Displacement effects can occur, with business being drained away from some areas or destinations because of the drawing power, or disruptions caused by events. ■ Evaluators will have to separate business sponsors from others when examining impacts, and the 'free-loader' phenomena has to be considered (i.e., some gain without contributing).
Sponsorship value: This can include agencies providing grants, and it depends on their goals – commercial or public service? Sponsors assess value in a number of ways (Michelini et al., 2017). ■ One approach for events is to determine the value of events as properties for investment and co-branding. In other words, how much will the 'title' and all other sponsors pay (or commit 'in-kind'/ 'contra') to the event? This is useful because a not-for-profit or public organisation can put a commercial value on the event.	■ Corporate data is often unavailable ■ How to place value on 'contra', or contributions 'in-kind' such as donated labour, marketing, product. ■ Events are seldom 'sold' on the open market ■ Sponsors might make contributions, expecting marketing and 'goodwill' benefits, while banks refuse to loan money to financially weak organisations
Sustainability value: Principles of 'sustainable development' can be applied to evaluating the worth of an event.	Ask these questions: did the event(s) make it more costly or difficult for future generations to enjoy an equal or better quality of life? Were irreplaceable resources used up? Do events add to global environmental problems, or help solve them? Could the long-term impacts be predicted and, where necessary, were preventative and ameliorative actions implemented?

2.6 Perspectives on event value

We see 'value' or 'worth' used in particular ways in the events and tourism literature, so we have been exploring the term in various contexts, summarized in the sequence of figures labeled "Value perspectives and challenges". Some key references are provided, and major evaluation challenges identified. The various perspectives do represent stakeholder perspectives to a degree, but of course stakeholders can be interested in any combination.

2.6.1 Evaluation and success

The meanings we give to 'success' are quite varied. The most widely accepted definition is that of achieving one's goals. A business-dominant culture puts value on events in ways that are different from a service-oriented culture. In business it is logical to equate success with operating profitability, share value, competitive advantage, a strong brand or even being bought out for a huge return on investment. Entrepreneurs can be 'successful' even in failure, being given credit for taking risks, innovating or 'changing the playing field'. These are all extrinsic measures of success, as someone else is assigning value, notably the consumer, the marketplace or the media.

'Public good' created by events and tourism is also a legitimate measure of success. And even if an event fails or loses money there can be recognition of its good works and changes brought to society or culture.

Is evaluation essential to success? Yes and no. It is NO in the sense that you can have a great event or business without planning, goals, or evaluation, either by luck or skill. People do not normally set out, however, to achieve success without a plan. It is a YES in the sense that a learning organisation, integrating evaluation in all its operations, has a better chance of surviving, prospering and attaining its goals.

Study questions

1   Define 'worth' and 'merit' in the context of event evaluation and explain the roles of the evaluator on making these determinations.

2   Compare intrinsic and extrinsic value perspectives with reference to key event and tourism stakeholders.

3   Cities invest a great deal in events and venues for events, but is it justified? Discuss the conditions you feel should be met in the event and event-tourism policy fields to justify interventions of different types.

Recommended additional readings and resources

Encyclopedia of Evaluation (2005). Edited by: Sandra Mathison. Sage.

The SAGE Handbook of Evaluation (2006). Edited by: Ian F. Shaw, Jennifer C. Greene & Melvin M. Mark. Sage.

The Value of Events (2017). Edited by: Lundberg, E., Armbrecht, J., Andersson, T., & Getz, D. Abingon, UK: Routledge.

The Routledge Handbook of Events (2012). Edited by: Stephen Page & Joanne Connell. Abingdon, UK: Routledge.

Routledge Handbook of Sports Event Management (2015). Edited by: Milena Parent & Jean-Loup Chappelet. Abingdon, UK: Routledge.

3 Theory

3.1 Introduction

Several theoretical perspectives are covered in this chapter, but first it is necessary to understand what is meant by 'theory'. Here are two standard dictionary definitions:

A system of ideas intended to explain something, based on general principles.

A set of principles on which the practice of an activity is based.

A good scientific theory can both explain and predict with certainty, but these kinds of theories are not found in management or social studies. Instead, we have systems of ideas, and sometimes these ideas are best described as 'theory fragments' and not a coherent whole. We can also talk about principles or propositions, based on thought and research, that can guide management. Sometimes in concluding a research paper I will put forward a set of propositions that I believe are warranted, and these propositions can either be used to guide management or further research.

You can also think of theory as a construct, model, or a conceptual framework that helps us understand the real world. This chapter starts with 'theories of evaluation', meaning organised thought and propositions or principles about the conduct of evaluation. My own contribution to theory development follows, being a model to illustrate a 'continuum of complexity' with specific reference to event and tourism evaluation. Then consideration is given to evidence and proof, what they mean and how evaluators might want one or the other depending on circumstances; this is an important elaboration of theories of evaluation. Systems theory is introduced in order to highlight internal and external perspectives on event evaluation and the importance of stakeholders.

3.2 Theories of evaluation

There are theories that can *guide* evaluation (i.e., theory-driven) and theories *of* evaluation. Evaluation theorists Alkin and Christie (2004) and Christie and Alkin (2008) argued that evaluation theory has its roots in both 'systematic social inquiry' and the need for 'social accountability and fiscal control'. They distinguish between theorists who emphasize one of three branches: 1) methods (largely concerned with validity and hence control groups, experiments and quasi-experiments, statistical analysis, and the generalizability of results that helps create knowledge); 2) how evaluation is used and by whom; and 3) the concept and practice of valuing. The following quotations from Christie and Alkin (2008) demonstrate how they view evaluation theories:

> (p. 131) *Our view is that there are three basic elements in considering evaluation theories: use, methods, and valuing. All theorists are concerned with the methods that will be employed in conducting the evaluation. All theorists recognize that evaluation is an enterprise that involves valuing (distinguishing it from most research). All theorists recognize that evaluations will be used in ways that affect programmes.*

> (p. 132) *While the term theory is conventionally used in the evaluation literature, it is more appropriate to use the terms approaches, models, or even frameworks.*

Here is what evaluation theory does, in a nutshell, in the context of events. Note the specific references to methods, uses and valuing.

♦ Advises on how to construct knowledge about events and event tourism.

♦ Advises on how to assign value to events, event tourism, and related performance issues.

♦ Informs about the nature of what we evaluate (paradigms, purposes, objects of evaluation).

◆ Suggests how to use the knowledge gained by evaluation for practice (i.e., problem-solving and decision-making) and theory development about events and event tourism.

◆ Sets standards for how evaluators should practice and for valid evaluations.

3.2.1 Methods

Looking specifically at methods in evaluation theory, there are some terms that need to be explained.

Theory-driven evaluations start with theory about how interventions should produce desired results, then usually employ experiments and quasi-experiments to prove cause and effect. In turn, the evaluations aid in theory development, as we can never have a perfect understanding of how humans and organisations behave. We do occasionally see event and tourism evaluations based on theories (e.g., to test the hypothesis that event production, attendance or volunteering generates social capital), but we see little or no effort to utilize experimental designs or even field experiments to prove cause and effect.

Evaluation theorists stress randomization in sampling and control groups for experimental designs, but these are not generally found in event impact assessments or other evaluations. Random sampling is desired for any visitor survey, but seldom achieved, so a reliance on systematic sampling is the norm, and often that level of reliability is not achieved.

Goals (or objectives) oriented evaluations attempt to demonstrate that goals were attained. The goals might be political, theory-based, or just based on wishful thinking. This is the most common model, and the one favoured in this book as reflected in the Event Compass and the overall emphasis on goals and key performance indicators. But it comes with an important caveat: for evaluations impact assessments of all kinds, it is necessary to avoid tunnel vision.

Goals-free evaluation is done by external experts, without knowledge or reference to stated organisational goals. The aim is to be completely objective in determining what a policy, programme or event actually does and the outcomes – not merely looking at the question of whether or not stated goals were attained. This has the advantage of potentially uncovering externalities and undesired outcomes. Far too many evaluations and impact assessments are narrowly focused (i.e., tunnel vision) and therefore miss important costs and negative impacts, or ignore distributional effects.

Realist evaluation: this approach derives from critical theory or critical realism, is in deliberate opposition to most forms of empirical evaluation methods, and has been advocated for complex social interventions. Social and political context must be considered in evaluating programme, policy or event effectiveness. For example, events might lead to desired social integration and community development, but for some, not all. This quotation is from the website Better Evaluation (http://www.betterevaluation.org):

"*Pawson & Tilley (1997) describe the procedure followed in the implementation of realist evaluation techniques in programme evaluation and emphasise that once hypotheses have been generated and data collected, the outcomes of the programme are explored, focusing on the groups that the programme benefitted and those who did not benefit. Effectiveness of a programme is thus not dependent on the outcomes alone (cause–effect), rather there is a consideration of the theoretical mechanisms that are applied, and the socio-historical context in which the programmes were implemented. Thus, the final explanation of a programme considers context-mechanism-outcome.*"

3.2.2 Uses

Turning to uses, we have several approaches to consider.

Utilization-focused evaluation reflects Patton's (2008) view that an evaluation should be judged on its usefulness to its intended users. Stakeholders, especially the primary users of the evaluation, have to be engaged from the start, feel owner-ship, and their interests guide the entire evaluation process. The evaluator then facilitates decision-making by those stakeholders. They could be the event organisers, residents of a community, the tourism industry or perhaps a group of amateur athletes.

Developmental evaluation is an approach that resembles action research or R and D (research and development) within an organisation. It is intended to encourage and facilitate change or innovation and requires real-time feedback in a continuous planning/development loop. This approach might also be useful to events facing a crisis – asking the question: how can we survive this? Speed will be of the essence, and ideas will have to be tested and accepted or rejected in real time.

Participatory evaluation: It is similar to action research and the utilization-based approach in that stakeholders are engaged, and the proposed ultimate use guides the project. Stakeholders can become involved in forming the evaluation plan, determining the interventions (e.g., create an event) and predicting outputs and outcomes.

Empowerment evaluation is similar to community development in that an event, for example, is produced in order to provide a community with the tools and knowledge that enables them to monitor and evaluate their own performance. Fetterman et al. (2015) described it as the use of evaluation to foster improvement and self-determination.

Appreciative inquiry: Coming from organisational development theory (see Coghlan et al., 2003), this approach sees evaluation as a process intended to realize a vision or to continuously improve. Instead of looking at problems, the evaluators assess what is best, what works, and how more could be achieved. Event staff and volunteers can in this way talk about their positive experiences and how to move forward – as opposed to continuously looking at problems and costs, or failures and unintended impacts. This cannot realistically be done by ignoring costs and problems, but it is a form of positive-thinking evaluation.

3.2.3 CIPP model (Context, Input, Process and Product)

Stufflebeam's CIPP is a decision-focused evaluation model (in Kellaghan & Stufflebeam, 2003) that emphasises the systematic provision of information for management and decision support with the aim of continuous improvement. Evaluations are carried out in formative, process and summative stages. Here are some key questions related to CIPP:

Context: What needs to be done? (formative); were important needs addressed? (summative)

Input: How should it be done? and afterwards, was a defensible design employed?

Process: Is it being done? was the design well executed?

Product: Is it succeeding? did the effort succeed?

Figure 3.1 illustrates CIPP applied to a charity event. Each of the four quadrants requires establishment of on-going evaluation methods and indicators.

Figure 3.1: CIPP applied to a charity event, adapted from Stufflebeam, in Kellaghan & Stufflebeam (2003) .

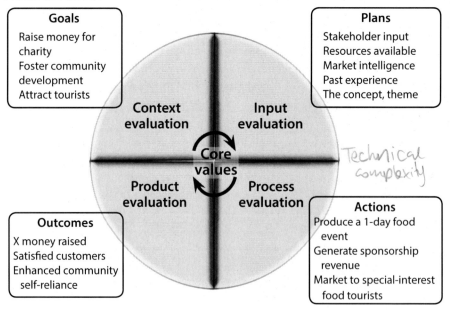

3.3 Continuum of event evaluation complexity

Figure 3.2 illustrates a number of important issues affecting the complexity of event evaluations. The horizontal axis represents technical complexity as defined by the amount of skill and effort required, and usually by the necessity for research versus other ways of getting evidence. Theory enters the picture when it becomes necessary to predict and evaluate cause and effect.

The vertical axis represents political complexity, taking into account the views and needs of various internal and external stakeholders and the political/governmental processes and regulations that affect planned events. Once an event opens up to the influence of external stakeholders, including sponsors and grant-givers, it sacrifices a degree of independence. The same holds true when event organisations form alliances, expand their scope to become tourist attractions, or partner with venues or other organisations. A number of environmental forces will act on events no matter what they do, such as the influence of competition and general economic forces, but these can be evaluated, and in part dealt with through higher-level strategies and partnerships of the kind that cities and destinations are increasingly forming.

This model has in large part shaped the need for two books, with this one focussing on the basic evaluation challenges facing event managers (below the dotted line) and the impact-related challenges covered in a companion book. The reality is that most event practitioners are not engaging in the higher-complexity applications.

Figure 3.2: Evaluation complexity model

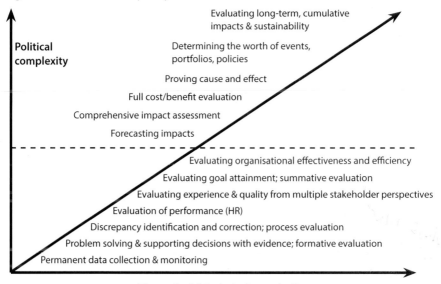

A permanent evaluation system will have data collection and monitoring as its base, because the absence of relevant data always impedes evaluation and planning. In general, this figure suggests that simple management problems, or questions that have to be answered are the least technically complex and likely have few if any political implications. But that is not always the case.

During recent consulting and speaking, practitioners from events and tourism have identified for me some of the many challenges that require, or affect evaluation. I have grouped them for easier interpretation, and they help shape the complexity continuum. There is no surprise in the emphasis on economic realities, but notice how practitioners stress the need for basic data, and even this task meets resistance. Both political reasons and the absence of resources often make the implementation of evaluation either unfeasible or unwanted. Politically (and this includes both government and internal management politics) evaluation is sometimes perceived to be dangerous!

a) Opposition to evaluation (could be politically motivated) or a belief it is unnecessary

b) Basic data collection and monitoring:
- Lack of staff or expertise to do it
- Cannot do real evaluation or impact assessment without good data
- Absence of state/nation-wide data for benchmarking
- Did we achieve all our goals? How to determine goal attainment
- How can we continuously improve our quality of service and performance?

c) Economic realities:
- Is there a simple, accurate, valid multiplier or forecasting model? Transparency, standardization and ease of use are important
- It is difficult to compare impact assessments; politics are at play; legitimacy is needed for methods
- Defining failure and success depends on politics
- Attracting real tourists and increasing their yield
- Assessing the risks and costs versus benefits
- Losing money
- Declining support
- What to re-invest?
- Convincing agencies to give grants
- How can we get more for our money?
- Did our various management units use their resources efficiently?
- Competition among cities and events
- Time, staff and money constraints on collecting data or doing evaluations
- Weather is a threat

d) Growth and sustainability:
- How to create sustainable growth?
- Getting any growth at all!
- Defining sustainability for events and event tourism

e) Marketing and visitors:
- Making marketing more effective, especially social media
- Bad publicity from incidents
- Were our visitors satisfied?

◆ How to measure "feel good" reactions (same as satisfaction?)

f) Community relations:

◆ Engaging the community (e.g., as volunteers, for support);

◆ Showing benefits to the community

◆ Getting local businesses to sponsor events

◆ Justifying events to the community (e.g., in light of inconveniences and costs)

◆ Resolving conflicting goals for the event (e.g., the organisers, the venue, other stakeholders)

◆ Measuring sociocultural outcomes

◆ Not meeting the expectations of community and other stakeholders

◆ Educating residents and politicians about events and tourism; getting community involved

As soon as impacts are considered, complexity increases greatly. The most basic economic impact assessment has to estimate new income for the destination attributable to the event, and requires visitor surveys, organisational data, and an impact calculator. Doing a comprehensive cost and benefit evaluations is very complex, including the necessity for employing surrogate measures such as resident perceptions of impacts and the issues surrounding opportunity costs, long-term depreciation or legacy value, and the need for triple-bottom-line accounting.

Determining the worth or value of an event becomes even more complex, both technically and politically. The highest levels of complexity on this diagram apply to portfolios and populations of events, particularly to evaluate their long-term, cumulative impacts, population health, and asset-value issues. Questions that arise: do we have a healthy and sustainable population of events in our city? what are all our events worth as portfolio assets? should we be bidding on mega events or developing more hallmark events? These are non-routine evaluation applications, probably not even considered in many cities and destinations. Strategic planning involving all the internal and external stakeholders will be needed to make certain that a comprehensive, long-term perspective is taken.

3.4 Evidence and proof

Let's start with a typical definition of 'proof' :

evidence or argument establishing or helping to establish a fact or the truth of a statement

Can you prove it? Evaluators will be asked that question, and it can be difficult to answer. Take the controversy surrounding mega events. Can proof be established through evidence or argument that hosting a mega event is good for a city or country, taking into account all costs and benefits? All too often a politically-motivated argument wins the day, whereas evaluators (and scientists) want really good evidence before they accept any proposition about costs and benefits. This is why so many evaluators want proof to be established through experimental designs that demonstrate clear cause and effect, whereas others accept that it is often impossible and unnecessary to employ experimental designs. In this way any discussion of evidence and proof is part of the 'theories of evaluation'.

Correlation studies: We often hear that X is associated with Y, based (when you look more closely) on correlation studies. In this statistical technique, changes in one variable are examined with regard to their fit with changes in another. But this in no way constitutes proof of cause and effect. It is evidence, but not conclusive. So, if you hear that there is a significant correlation between hosting mega events and a prosperous economy, do not believe it. Dig much deeper.

Now consider standard definitions of 'evidence':

1. *A thing or set of things helpful in forming a conclusion or judgment.*

2. *Something indicative; an indication or set of indications.*

3. *The means by which an allegation may be proven, such as oral testimony, documents, or physical objects.*

There are many forms of evidence available to evaluators, and basically it is up to the evaluators and stakeholders to decide what evidence is pertinent, obtainable and compelling in making judgements. This can be a political issue, as important decisions involving investments will only be taken (we hope) when there is sound evidence that governments create public good, or private profit (for investors) will be realised.

And when you consider the 'continuum of complexity', some decisions will require a very high level of proof, necessitating multiple forms of convincing evidence.

In programme evaluation the emphasis is often placed on proving that programmes cause the effects they were intended to, or in other words that the goals have been met and can be attributed to the programme itself. This 'burden of proof' is often going to be impossible in the world of events and tourism.

What are facts? Dictionaries define 'fact' in these ways:

1. *a thing that is indisputably the case*

2. *a piece of information used as evidence or as part of a report or news article*

3. *the truth about events as opposed to interpretation*

Establishing the 'truth' might depend more on the credibility of the evaluator, or the bias of a decision maker, than the nature of the information. For example, one expert claims that it is 'a fact' that building arenas for professional sport teams is good for the economy because they attract tourists and investors, while another says that argument (often heard when major public investment is sought by private team owners) is (a) false because it is based on poor research and (b) deliberately misleading because it fails to consider opportunity costs and the distribution of costs and benefits. Whom will the decision makers listen to?

Most evaluations are designed to obtain facts, some of which can be used as evidence in drawing conclusions or assigning worth. Evidence can be clear-cut and irrefutable, such as: "we all witnessed the accident and there is no doubt about the injury suffered", or subject to interpretation and dispute, such as "many people in the community think the event is disruptive and too expensive". How would you deal with each of those scenarios? What weight would you place on the evidence, whether factual or subjective in nature?

As evidence accumulates, for example that a portfolio of planned events is causing certain desired or undesired outcomes, then policies and strategies can be improved. This assumes that evidence is shared, reliable, and professionally assessed, and the whole process is transparent.

3.5 Systems theory and thinking systematically

What does it mean to be systematic? How is systems theory relevant to evaluation? These definitions are relevant:

1. System: a set of connected things or parts forming a complex whole, in particular a set of things working together as parts of a mechanism or an interconnecting network

2. System: a set of principles or procedures according to which something is done; an organised scheme or method

The first definition applies to an event when conceptualized as a complex, interacting set of people, management and setting. In *systems theory* the event is a *transforming process.*

That takes *inputs* (resources, information, ideas) and generates *outputs* and *outcomes* (such as happy customers, or economic impacts). Also theoretical is the understanding that such a system is *open* – that is, it depends upon inputs from its environment and it in turn influences environmental conditions.

Definition 2, above, can either refer to a normative approach to management, in the form of a set of principles like 'corporate social responsibility' or 'sustainable development', or to any framework such as our 'continuum of evaluation complexity' that is intended to help managers. This also applies to an evaluation system such as the 'Event Compass'.

3.5.1 A systems model

Figure 3.3 is a model illustrating how the organisation (either an event or agency) is a part of the community and the larger environment, and how internal management functions must be inter-dependent to function as a whole. External evaluation is undertaken by stakeholders (including certifying organisations, funders, regulators) while internal evaluation is part of normal management. 'Outputs' are the expected results, such as attendance, revenue, customer satisfaction. 'Outcomes' or 'impacts' are sometimes differentiated from outputs and described as longer-term or permanent changes and are not normally part of a single event's goals – except perhaps for occasional mega-events.

Figure 3.3: A systems model

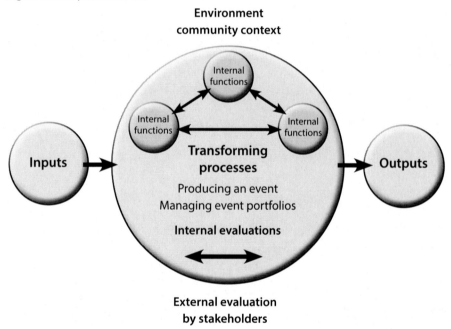

Managers must think systematically about their organisation, its strategy, and evaluation, while a systematic approach to evaluation means it is comprehensive, permanent, linked to strategy and goals, triple-bottom-line in orientation but also considers externalities and unintended outcomes.

Reflexive professionals always consider why and what they are doing in the context of fulfilling their responsibilities, achieving goals, and adhering to sustainability principles. It is dangerous to fall into the habit of compartmentalised thinking, only considering one's narrow area of functional responsibility. Changes in organisational culture might be required to get managers into this systematic frame of mind.

The systems approach is not really a method, but rather a framework within which appropriate and necessary methods can be determined. The model requires consideration of various levels of environment and therefore potentially numerous stakeholders, of inputs including resources and information of value, of management processes and their interdependencies, and of outcomes related to both internal processes and externalities. With the event conceived as a transforming process, the systematic evaluator will automatically take a more comprehensive and open-minded view of what evaluation is to achieve and how it is to be conducted.

3.5.2 Internal and external evaluations

Within a systems approach to event management or event tourism, both internal and external evaluation processes are essential (see Getz, 2012, 2013). Internal evaluation is a standard management function, usually undertaken by senior managers or owners, and often supported by a routine technical process of gathering and analyzing data.

Evaluation is also conducted externally, sometimes as a planned input to event operations and sometimes independently. As events have become legitimized as tools for a wide range of public policies and corporate or industry strategies, many stakeholders are evaluating their investments and interventions in the event sector. This trend has resulted in demands for increased accountability to multiple stakeholders and their particular criteria, making the manager's evaluation tasks both complex and politically charged. To fully explore this complexity requires consideration of stakeholder theory and related event-specific research (e.g., Larson and Wikstrom, 2001; Mossberg and Getz, 2006; Crespi-Vallbona and Richards, 2007; Getz et al., 2007; Parent and Seguin, 2007; Andersson and Getz, 2008; Leopkey and Parent, 2009; Larson, 2009; Prebensen, 2010; Ziakas, 2013; Harris, 2014).

Participatory evaluation (discussed earlier, p.28) according to Derrett (2015:276), is appropriate for many planned events in that it involves stakeholders and thereby builds trust and supports sustainability of the event. Making it work could involve stakeholder surveys, the internalization of key stakeholders onto boards of directors or advisory boards, or open forums in the community. This of course opens up the event to potential criticism and having to deal with complaints, but it is also an exercise in accountability. Open participatory evaluation is one method to assess values and obtain opinions on the overall perception of the event, including its value creation and general worth.

Transparency has also become an issue. While many event owners and managers might prefer to conduct their evaluations in secret, or event-tourism development agencies might seek to avoid public scrutiny altogether, it is definitely in the interest of the public and many other stakeholders to insist upon an open and standardized evaluation process. This tendency is most pronounced when government support is critical, as in supporting festivals or bidding on events, because the intervention has to be politically justified.

External stakeholders often want to conduct their own evaluations, related to their purposes in being involved, although they might insist that the research be done by the organisers. This can be complicated, especially for authorities (typically local governments) that both support and regulate events and venues. Some external stakeholders will be content with valuing the event solely from the perspective of their investment (so that goal attainment and/or ROI measures will be compiled) while others will want to get involved in (or require) more detailed evaluations of management systems. For example, sponsors and grant-giving bodies often demand the production and submission of financial accounts, visitor surveys, evidence of meeting branding conditions (e.g, were logos properly displayed) and much more. Accordingly, evaluation systems generally require very careful consideration of all stakeholder positions.

Consensus building is a process intended to resolve conflicts or to plan within a complex stakeholder environment. Evaluation is often like that, especially when the aim is to decide if an event is worthy of creation or continuation, or where value lies in a portfolio of events. Collaboration is needed, with stakeholders willing to compromise when necessary for the group to resolve the issue. If stakeholders are intractable, keeping to their position no matter what, the group can still reach a partial (or majority-based) decision, but implementation might prove difficult. Some stakeholders will be more important than others, for example holding the power that comes from money, and others might form into voting blocks to achieve more influence.

Study questions

1   Explain the difference between theories of evaluation (elaborate on use, methods, value) and theory-based evaluation (give an example).

2   How does thinking systematically aid the evaluator, particularly when it comes to involving stakeholders? Include an illustration of a systems model for an event.

3   Why is cost-benefit evaluation more complex than evaluation to solve a particular problem for event managers? Explain how complexity is related to politics, and what the evaluator must do to meet the complexity challenge.

Recommended additional readings and sources

Better Evaluation (http://www.betterevaluation.org)

Derrett, R. (2015). *The Complete Guide to Creating Enduring Festivals.* New York: Wiley.

Kellaghan, T. & Stufflebeam, D. (Eds.)(2003). *International Handbook of Educational Evaluation.* Springer.

4 A Model of the Evaluation Process

Learning objectives

☐ Understand the major considerations in the evaluation process.

☐ Know the main evaluation paradigms (positivistic; interpretive; critical/emancipatory) and their implications.

☐ Be aware of how context influences evaluation, including formal versus informal and internal versus external.

☐ Understand the purposes of evaluation within event management and event tourism, including problem solving, supporting decisions and providing evidence of goal attainment.

☐ Learn the specific topics or problems associated with formative, process and summative evaluations.

☐ Differentiate between outputs and outcomes.

☐ Understand the uses of evaluation are not always in line with stated purpose.

☐ Learn how to maximise the utility of evaluation.

4.1 Introduction

In this chapter a general model of the evaluation process is discussed, with a focus on issues and challenges for event and tourism evaluators. This is not about how to plan or design an evaluation project (the subject of the ensuing chapter) but the main things evaluators have to consider before even beginning an evaluation: paradigms and theories, the "why evaluate?" question, what to evaluate, and ultimate uses of evaluations. 'Measures' and 'methods' are illustrated in the model but are discussed more fully in the next chapter.

4.2 A model of the evaluation process

The diagram (Figure 4.1) provides a summary of the ensuing discussion on the major elements of the study of event evaluation. It begins with three evaluation paradigms that underpin any discussion of evaluation and apply to all applications. Most evaluations are of the routine, problem-solving kind and are low on technical and theoretical complexity; they do not require much thought about philosophy, politics or theory. But as complexity increases, particularly when different values and stakeholder perspectives come into plan – as in cost and benefit evaluation – then consideration of paradigms becomes important.

Figure 4.1: Major considerations in the evaluation process

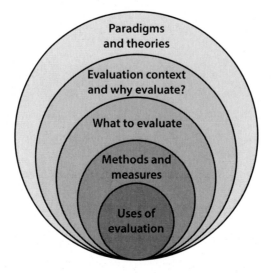

4.3   Evaluation paradigms

Read this section in conjunction with the previous discussion of evaluation theory.

Paradigms can be thought of as a guiding model, and in science they are a set of concepts, theories, research methods, postulates, and standards that define legitimate research. As such, they are open to debate and preference.

The *positivist paradigm* dominates event and tourism evaluation, notably through the prevailing emphasis on measuring economic impacts, customer satisfaction, and other quantifiable outcomes. According to Rossi et al. (2004) it includes needs assessment, assessment of programme theory and process, and efficiency. When evaluators search for the truth (as in "we can prove it") they are falling into this paradigm, whereas when they search for relevance and consensus they might be tending towards an *interpretive paradigm*.

A set of 'interpretive' approaches has been described by Potter (2006), and these have in common an attempt to work with stakeholders to understand their expectations, experiences and meanings before making judgment about value or worth. Close links with stakeholders and the community at large will obviously facilitate interpretive event evaluation, with specific qualitative methods including focus groups, interviews and observation. This paradigm is likely to be more appropriate in evaluating event populations, policies, and legacies, all of which are open to various interpretations of cumulative impacts and values. Wood (2009a:183) put forward a framework for the evaluation of festival impacts that can be considered interpretive in design.

A third paradigm is that of *critical-emancipatory evaluation* (Potter, 2006) which is usually based on action research. The aim is to make changes, or initiate transformative processes, such as to employ events in community capacity building through institutional networking, or to facilitate healthy lifestyles and participation in the arts or sport. Where the aim is to empower citizens or groups, the process can be quite political and controversial, especially if existing power structures are challenged.

The *interpretive evaluation paradigm* leads to the involvement of stakeholders in the process, sometimes called '*participatory evaluation*'. The first step is to ask who wants to be involved, although if the event or agency is already actively managing its stakeholder relationships this should be automatic. Others might want to be involved, especially if they have a grievance, requiring some determination of their claims to legitimacy.

Beyond being an exercise in programme or event evaluation, wider goals might be relevant. This type of stakeholder engagement can be used in community development to empower residents or groups, thereby building capacity and hopefully support. Building networks in this way can add to mutual understanding and overall knowledge of issues. On the other hand, there will be additional time and cost requirements and the risk of failure. In some cases conflict resolution might be needed to sort out competing interests.

True collaboration will be required, because this approach asks those involved to relinquish control and seek consensus on the purpose, goals, methods and uses of the evaluation. If it works well, the evaluation or impact assessment should have a greater chance of leading to real change. In this way, it is a tool in 'action research'.

The paradigms discussed above do not directly suggest methodology or methods of evaluation. Indeed mixed methods drawing from a number of disciplines can be used no matter what the underlying philosophy.

While *methods* are used to solve problems or obtain facts and evidence, *methodology* provides the underlying rationale. Evaluators who seek to prove that an event causes a desired outcome (i.e., they want to establish cause and effect) might use an experimental method within the positivistic paradigm. Methodologies are theory and paradigm-based approaches to doing research, and they are often associated with, but not 'owned by' certain academic disciplines. In sociology, for example, both quantitative and qualitative methods are employed, and both the interpretive and positivistic paradigms have their adherents.

4.4   Evaluation contexts – why evaluate?

Consider the ensuing list of contexts in which evaluation might be done. Context often determines, or at least influences, why evaluations are done, and how.

♦ Formal (e.g., for accountability) vs. informal (e.g., a quick, easy study)

♦ Internal vs. external (collaborative and open, or internal and secret?)

♦ Formative, process or summative?

♦ Monitoring and data collecting, or is original research needed?

♦ Goal attainment or goals-free?

♦ For a one-time event (a project), or for periodic events and strategic in nature?

♦ Certification needed (i.e., for sustainability), or to support routine decisions

♦ Single event oriented, or for an entire portfolio?

♦ Technical (problem solving), or to evaluate worth/merit?

Textbooks often incorporate evaluation into planning and programming models, and in relation to events this often means project planning, especially for one-time events. In this context the evaluation will likely be formal and goal-driven. Performance objectives or key performance indicators generally accompany this approach. Informal evaluation occurs when people get together to discuss issues, plan for improvements or solve problems without having done research or installed an evaluation system. 'Goal-free evaluation' is always an option, but likely to be implemented only when there is a need for a completely objective evaluation of processes and impacts (usually conducted by outsiders) that might reveal more than a goal-driven process.

Success is quite different from long-term sustainability. When a project is completed according to specifications, within the budget and on schedule, that is success. One-time events are traditionally evaluated in that way with the proviso that mega-events are now expected to generate a positive, long-term legacy that also needs to be evaluated. Periodic events might have a planned life cycle (i.e., they are intended to be produced only a few times) while others seek permanence or sustainability.

Permanence means *forever*, as valued traditions and institutions (see Andersson and Getz, 2008; Getz and Andersson, 2008), whereas to 'be *sustainable*' has come to mean compliance with a set of norms. Sustainability will always be a moving target, with planning and evaluation for sustainability requiring commitment to continuous improvement through evaluation and learning systems.

Typical internal evaluations, conducted by and for management, can range from very specific goal-attainment exercises, such as monitoring customer satisfaction, to broad, ongoing evaluations of efficiency and effectiveness across all management functions. They need not involve stakeholders and might never be reported outside the organisation. Some events are very independent and inward-looking, so their entire evaluation universe consists of ways to improve and sustain the event. The event, in this context, exists for its own sake and might not be conceived as an instrument of any external policy or strategy. Nevertheless, internal evaluation cannot ignore environmental influences, especially those affecting resource acquisition.

External evaluations are conducted from the perspective of stakeholders who evaluate the event and its organisation, and are conducted either by outside agents or by event managers who are held accountable for resources and support received. Sponsors and grant-givers often insist upon full evaluations or at least impact assessments, and many will conduct their own ROI-type evaluations of events they support; these are not necessarily made public. However, one can argue that adopting principles of social responsibility leads to a greater external orientation, as does increasing institutionalization of an event or the event-producing organisation (Getz and Andersson, 2008), thereby suggesting the need for transparent evaluations and full, public disclosure. The concept of a 'social license to operate' can be applied (Williams et al., 2007), in which case the event is seen to require ongoing community or key-stakeholder support.

Events are increasingly instruments of various industry strategies (both tourism and corporate marketing) and public-policy domains (from economic and urban development to place marketing and civic re-positioning). Accordingly, many large-scale, public events are in reality transforming processes designed (or expected) to achieve goals that lie outside an event's ability to control. This places a huge burden on events, and requires a completely different approach to evaluation – one that involves a partnership between events and stakeholders. For example, if festivals are expected to foster social integration in a divided community, then a huge problem of demonstrating cause and effect arises.

Evaluation of portfolios of events will be much more complex, starting with numerous environmental forces and stakeholders shaping the portfolio, reflecting an overriding concern for long-term and cumulative impacts, and leading to diverse perspectives on value as demonstrated through multiple evaluations and a wide variety of methods. Longitudinal, meta-analysis of a number of evaluation and impact studies might be required to gain the entire picture. Here are two big challenges:

♦ What is the event or portfolio worth in economic and subjective terms? Place an economic value through the application of various ROI and asset life-cycle accounting procedures. Make subjective judgments through comparisons, discourse, and stakeholder input.

♦ Is our event or portfolio/population of events healthy and sustainable? Use a variety of indicators to monitor cumulative impacts; measure population changes such as births and deaths.

Event evaluations are rare, if non-existent, in the context of the interpretive or critical-emancipatory paradigms, or as part of action research. This remains a frontier in event studies, in need of both theoretical and methodological advances.

Criticism of mega-events in particular has been growing, and the conflict over vast expenditures on sports events and facilities that benefit mostly powerful elites in society requires new approaches to evaluation of costs, benefits and overall worth.

Evaluation of events often has to consider long-term, indirect, and possibly subtle impacts. The term *'legacy'* applies to all that is left over from the event (or events) as a positive inheritance for future generations, or as costs and problems. For discussions of event 'legacies' see: Hall, 1994; Ritchie, 2000; Preuss, 2007; Quinn, 2010; Sadd, 2010. One can ask if an event itself is sustainable, or if its legacy fits into a sustainable development framework. Specific to mega-events, Hall (2012) concluded that they could not be considered sustainable, and that the dominant paradigm that has generated intense competition for mega-events must itself be altered.

4.5 Why evaluate?

Surprisingly little attention has been paid to the question of assigning overall value or worth to a planned event, let alone to portfolios and populations of events. In the for-profit sector, events are a business and the need to make profit is a given, so events have clear asset value in this context. In the not-for-profit sector, events are usually conceived as providing a necessary or worthwhile service to the community or a specific group, and therefore some measure of value such as attendance, or of legitimacy – such as political and other stakeholder support – is essential to their continuance. It is in the public sector, where events are produced or receive support from government, that a specific justification for intervention is necessary. All too often that justification is limited to purported tourism and economic benefits, whereas the dramatic rise in exploiting events as instruments of diverse policy purposes demands much broader justifications.

The technical purposes of event evaluation are much clearer and are widely implemented:

◆ To aid in planning/design/marketing; solve problems; clarify logic and goals

◆ To improve management systems

◆ To improve competitiveness; stay on track; be successful.

Outcome or impact assessment is part of this process, especially employing measures of quality, customer satisfaction and loyalty, and some calculation of return on investment is often desired. Both efficiency of resource acquisition and use, and effectiveness in goal attainment are commonly examined.

4.6 What to evaluate

The "what to evaluate?" question can also be approached by looking at three stages of evaluation, usually called formative, process and summative.

4.6.1 Formative evaluation

The results of any evaluation can influence future planning and decisions, which is the basic idea behind a learning organisation, but in project terms there is always a planning and needs/feasibility assessment stage. Here are some typical formative questions:

♦ **Is the event/programme needed?** Assessing the need for an event or programme is not an easy matter. Many events are designed as a social service, in which case the target market might be a particular group (e.g., the disadvantaged economically, seniors, children) or all residents of a city. How is need determined? Inputs can take the form of social, economic and demographic data, or surveys of stakeholders concerning their perceived need and propensity to consume. Need will almost always be a subjective and/or political determination.

♦ **Will it be feasible?** This is a complex issue, as feasibility can be a financial, political or technical consideration. Demand forecasting is often the key, but in other cases it depends on cost estimates. Meeting specifications is a central issue for sport event feasibility. A component of feasibility studies should be consideration of opportunity costs (i.e., what else can we do with our resources?). In the end, a better question might be: is it desirable given the forecast costs and benefits?

♦ **What should the event consist of?** Informing the design of a project so that it will be effective (e.g., is there a theory or business model that suggests a project will be effective? have adequate resources been provided? are there good examples to benchmark against?).

Just because something can be done does not mean it should be. Derrett (2015:334) suggested that new festivals should only be started if they can make a case based on uniqueness, a new, non-competitive market, a viable business case, funding, a champion, an appropriate time slot and location, and support from other festivals, cultural organisations and the public.

4.6.2 Process evaluation

The programme or event is up and running, but that does not mean the evaluator can relax. Some critical questions emerge and they often require an immediate response.

♦ **Are we on track to achieve our goals?** Determining whether the event, policy or project is on course, according to specifications, is the essence of process evaluation. It has to include close and detailed monitoring of implementation through such mechanisms as staff/volunteer observations, customer and participant feedback, and it has to include a process for fixing problems and seizing opportunities.

◆ **What problems have to be fixed? or issues dealt with?** All the training for critical incidents comes to the fore, plus the need for contingency planning, to deal with problems as they arise. Management must retain a degree of flexibility to enable quick and decisive reactions. All of this must be documented carefully for future reference.

◆ **Do opportunities arise that require an immediate response?** Something unexpected might occur that enables improvements, or an easier path to goal achievement, and these can only be determined through monitoring (e.g., analysing each day's numbers) and reflexive management (i.e., being tuned into the prospect of making positive changes).

Process evaluation can also be more long-term in its orientation:

◆ **Can we improve our processes?** Finding out how the organisation, event or programme could be improved in terms of efficiency (resource use) and effectiveness (goal attainment) should be a part of the monitoring process during an event. Financial and human-resource audits can provide input, and these have to be incorporated throughout all stages of planning and evaluation.

4.6.3 Summative evaluation (outputs, outcomes and impacts)

To avoid confusion over terminology we have to consider *outputs*, *outcomes* and *impacts*. We can use the three terms synonymously, but evaluators have to consider a number of important factors:

◆ There are always intended consequences of events and tourism, including things like making a profit, satisfying customers, and attracting tourists who spend lots of money.

◆ There are often unintended consequences such as causing accidents, damaging the environment directly or through carbon emissions, or displacing poor people from their affordable housing.

◆ *Externalities* are costs borne by others, such as security costs or amenity losses not accounted for by the event organisers or tourism agencies.

◆ Long-term or permanent changes attributable to the event or events, such as changes in the economy and environment, are seldom attributable to one event – but have to be considered in terms of sustainable development. Cumulative impact assessment is difficult and rare.

◆ Impacts are often perceived or felt by residents and other stakeholders, even if they lack evidence of cause and effect.

All too often summative evaluations deal exclusively with goal attainment questions, such as did we achieve our targets? But in a systems approach all outcomes and impacts have to be considered, including those not desired (negatives) and those unexpected consequences that might be deemed good, bad or neutral. To find the unexpected and undesired requires going beyond goal attainment.

Here are some key questions that apply to summative evaluations:

♦ **Was the effort/expenditure/policy worthwhile taking into account all costs and benefits?** This is the ultimate evaluation question, going well beyond technical problem solving and continuous improvement. It is easy to pass judgement on an event when it fails financially or generates a lot of bad publicity, but how is success defined? And within a portfolio of events? Or in terms of sustainability goals?

♦ **Who gained and who paid?** It is not usual for evaluators to assess the distribution of costs and benefits, and indeed this issue is often deliberately ignored for political reasons. When economic impact analysis concludes that millions of new dollars entered the economy attributable to the event the evaluator should ask who gained from that revenue and who paid or suffered because of it?

♦ **Can we improve the quality of our products and services?** Get evidence through benchmarking, and by measuring the satisfaction of stakeholders and the importance they attach to specific products and services.

♦ **Are there better alternatives?** Estimating opportunity costs will assist in this decision. Find out what others are doing; conduct feasibility studies and do cost-benefit forecasts.

♦ **Are the event or programme goals appropriate and useful?** Compared to what? according to whom? These questions can usually only be answered subjectively or through a political process.

♦ **What is the event or portfolio worth in economic and subjective terms?** Place an economic value through the application of various ROI and asset life-cycle accounting procedures. Subjective judgements can be made through comparisons, discourse, or stakeholder input.

♦ **Is our event or portfolio/population of events healthy and sustainable?** Use a variety of indicators to monitor cumulative impacts; measure population changes such as births and deaths.

4.7 Uses

It should seem obvious that the up-front reasons for doing evaluation dictate the uses to which results are put. But sometimes evaluations are shelved and forgotten, put to the wrong uses, or were crafted with hidden uses in mind. Rossi et al. (2004:416) commented on the utilisation of evaluations and advised the following:

♦ Evaluators must understand the cognitive styles of decision makers

♦ Evaluation results must be timely and available when needed

♦ Evaluations must respect stakeholders' programme commitments

♦ Utilization and dissemination plans should be part of the evaluation design

♦ Evaluations should include an assessment of utilization.

Not only does use have to be planned, it is also up to the evaluators to ensure that they make results useful to all stakeholders. In goal-free and cost-benefit evaluations there might be some uncertainty about what to do with conclusions about unanticipated effects, external impacts and various interpretations of who benefits and who pays, as these are very complex issues. So its best to give thought to these eventualities at the outset.

4.7.1 Tourism-specific considerations

In discussing event tourism there is generally an implicit theoretical model at work – that events will attract tourists, and that their incremental spending (i.e., new money or export revenue) will generate economic benefits for the destination. Often the estimated economic impact, generally exaggerated through the application of income or value-added multipliers, will be considered as the ROI for development and tourism agencies that invested in the event. While this application is not necessarily part of an evaluation, it can be an input to placing a value on events or improving performance in event tourism.

First, economic benefits are not achieved without costs, and major developmental expenditures should be subject to consideration of opportunity costs. Second, many externalities are associated with events and tourism, including pollution, consumption of resources, amenity loss and sometimes social or cultural disruption. Third, the distribution of costs and benefits is of great importance, especially for major events. Evaluation requires taking all these factors into account to arrive at a reasoned conclusion about value (measured tangibly) and worth. When we say that something has worth, or is worthwhile, it is a justification for action.

Event tourism is instrumentalist, that is to say that events have a number of roles to play in tourism promotion and economic development: attraction, animator of venues and places, catalyst for additional development, image making and place marketing (Getz, 2013). Whether or not event-tourism strategy and management achieves these goals is the primary evaluation question, but there is also a host of secondary issues regarding the efficiency of the process (e.g., what kinds of events are best? how to measure ROI? how are event portfolios best managed?) and the need to consider unexpected and negative outcomes. The latter issue is considered in the companion book on impact assessment.

Evaluation of event tourism is not well developed, and it has been hampered by a pre-occupation with simplistic and often misleading economic impact forecasts and assessments. Full cost-benefit evaluations are seldom undertaken. Negative impacts and external costs are often ignored.

Study questions

1 Discuss the philosophical and ethical issues involved in the three evaluation paradigms, with reference to planned events.

2 Explain formative, process and summative evaluation and their relevance to (a) starting a new event and (b) planning for event tourism in a city.

Recommended additional readings and sources

EvaluationWiki.org

Rossi, P., Freeman, H. & Lipsey, M. (2004) *Evaluation: A Systematic Approach* (7th ed.). Thousand Oaks, CA: Sage.

socialresearchmethods.net

5 Measures, Methods and Planning an Evaluation Project

Learning objectives

☐ Be able to determine the data needed and appropriate data collection methods for evaluation.

☐ Know the meaning and uses of indicators and key performance indicators.

☐ Understand the need for both quantitative and qualitative methods and measures.

☐ Know the evaluation approaches or models that are available.

☐ Be able to plan a simple evaluation.

☐ Be able to plan a complex evaluation employing theory or logic models.

5.1 Introduction

Measures and methods become critical considerations when planning an evaluation project. Following from the discussion of a process model (paradigms, contexts, purposes and uses) this chapter looks first at measures, including the development and use of key performance indicators, than methodological issues and evaluation models. The final part provides step-by-step guidance on how to plan both simple and complex evaluations, with emphasis on the 'logic model'.

5.2 Measures

5.2.1 Indicators and key performance indicators

It is not always possible to measure something directly. For example, how do you measure quality, or sustainability? Evaluators employ indicators that reflect the essence of the concept, so when we need evidence of quality we can measure customer satisfaction or employ expert judges. In the case of sustainability, numerous indicators have been developed to measure everything from carbon emissions to habitat loss (see: http://www.sustainablemeasures.com). Here is a definition and criteria from that website:

"An indicator is something that points to an issue or condition. Its purpose is to show you how well a system is working. If there is a problem, an indicator can help you determine what direction to take to address the issue. Indicators are as varied as the types of systems they monitor. However, there are certain characteristics that effective indicators have in common:

♦ *Effective indicators are **relevant**; they show you something about the system that you need to know.*

♦ *Effective indicators are **easy to understand**, even by people who are not experts.*

♦ *Effective indicators are **reliable**; you can trust the information that the indicator is providing.*

♦ *Lastly, effective indicators are based on **accessible data**; the information is available or can be gathered while there is still time to act."*

Of all the possible indicators, some are considered to be critical. These can be called critical indicators or, when they are intended to measure performance (as in progress towards attaining goals) they can be called *key performance indicators* (KPIs). Since they will be situation specific, and subject to change, each organisation or event will have to formulate their own.

From a business perspective here is a definition of key performance indicators:

"Key business statistics such as number of new orders, cash collection efficiency, and return on investment (ROI), which measure a firm's performance in critical areas. KPIs show the progress (or lack of it) toward realizing the firm's objectives or strategic plans by monitoring activities which (if not properly performed) would likely cause severe losses or outright failure."

Source: http://www.businessdictionary.com/definition/key-performance-indicators-KPI.html

In this book I use 'KPI' to describe both direct measures, as in the key business statistics, and indirect indicators of concepts like sustainability. Terms that are more or less equivalent are performance measures and objectives.

KPIs are needed for all management functions, and there are five general types:

1 **Effectiveness**: implements the mission/mandate; goal attainment; priorities

2 **Efficiency**: use of resources; justifying costs; consider alternatives

3 **Relevance**: conformity to policy; perspectives of target groups and other stakeholders

4 **Sustainability** of the event, including its financial viability

5 **Impacts**: changes caused; totality of effects; distribution of costs and benefits.

KPIs can be categorized in several ways that will help determine which ones are key, and which are merely metrics to monitor. Some are *short-term* in nature, intended to deal with immediate objectives like: are we achieving our ticket-sales targets? When do we reach the break-even point?" Others are *longer-term* in orientation, such as: "do our satisfied customers become repeat visitors? Do residents continue to support our event?"

It will also be useful to determine which metrics (i.e., how things are measured) produce definitive answers, or merely provide some evidence towards reaching a conclusion. If most customers say they dislike the event experience and say they will not recommend it or return, those could be interpreted, collectively, as *definitive indicators* of failure!

Another categorization relates indicators to the three evaluation phases of formative, process and summative. *Formative indicators* will help plan the event or improve it in the future, such as monitoring trends in repeat versus first-time customers. The logic here is that if you only attract loyal repeaters your future audience is not being developed. You also want *early warning indicators* that might suggest future problems, such as a rising level of dissatisfaction, or declining visitor expenditure.

In the process evaluation phase, while the event is up and running, key indicators will be those that immediately identify problems to fix (e.g., accidents, complaints) or opportunities, such as increasing sales of merchandise or pleasantly surprising guests. Summative evaluation requires a set of KPIs related to each area of the triple bottom line, from economic impacts to meeting green or sustainability standards.

5.3 Methodology and methods

Methodologies can be understood in the context of paradigms, as previously discussed.

1 A body of rules and postulates that are employed by researchers in a discipline of study

2 A particular procedure or set of procedures

3 The analysis of the principles of procedures of inquiry that are followed by researchers in a discipline of study.

(source: what-when-how.com/social-sciences/methodology-social-science/)

Method: The strategies and tools used to obtain and analyse data or evidence. These might follow from evaluation theory, the paradigms, or disciplinary preferences. They range in sophistication and difficulty from laboratory experiments to monitoring energy consumption. Methods have to fit the evaluation problem at hand, and when we incorporate various research or data collection methods into an evaluation project we are really creating an evaluation model.

There is no *a priori* reason to exclude any qualitative or quantitative method from evaluation, and a range of each has to be part of the evaluator's 'toolbox'. When evaluation project planning is discussed later in this chapter we will look at some specific qualitative and quantitative methods.

5.4 Data and data collection

Data is not just numbers and stats! Data also means facts or evidence upon which analyses or reasoning can be made. Evaluators will collect data in many ways: from the standard visitor survey, stakeholder opinions, systematic analyses of interviews, content analysis of blogs, or facts extracted from official documents and other records. Systematic analysis of videos generates data, but to be useful in evaluation, data must be generated through reliable methods, without bias, and made available in a form that can be readily computed or evaluated.

By way of example, take observations made by volunteers at events. Their input is qualitative; it is raw data, unprocessed and not coded. But when generated through systematic observation, the observations become datum (i.e., specific bits of information) that can be analysed. Interviews can generate important insights, but there are methods of content analysis that will turn unconnected statements or even verbal ramblings into useful data.

Figures are provided throughout the book listing goals and related evaluation questions, KPIs, and data sources plus methods, for various evaluation purposes. These constitute the Evaluator's Toolbox and evaluators can customize these to their specific needs.

The first toolbox topic is for the most contemporary of data collection challenges – websites and social-media. However, the starting point is generic content analysis.

Figure 5.1: Evaluator's Toolbox: Content, website and social-media analysis

	Technique

Content analysis: a term that describes any form of objective, systematic, quantifiable analysis of content.
 	
Applications:
 	
■ Determine general trends that might affect tourism and events.
 	
■ Find out what people are saying about your event or destination.
 	
■ Evaluate media coverage: is it positive: fair; complete?
 	
■ Assess the effectiveness of your communications.
	1: Select the sources to be evaluated (e.g., newspaper articles, blogs, TV programmes).
	
	2: Determine what you are looking for:
	  (a) specific words, phrases, pictures, numbers
	  (b) ideas, values, concepts, symbols, themes, etc. that require deeper analysis; most challenging is assessing relationships among concepts, such as how people talk about an event when they are comparing event experiences on the basis of special leisure interests
	
	3: Coding, according to set rules, is necessary to reduce content to data that can be analysed; the text can suggest codes, or start with theory or expectations of content
	
	4: Reliability has to be checked, typically by using two or more trained coders
	
	5: Validity can be checked through focus groups, interviews, and other qualitative methods

Website analysis: Researchers confirm that an event's website is often the single-most important source of information for potential attendees. Google Analytics is one readily-available tool; it can collect data on: ■ How many people visit a website ■ Where users live ■ Websites that send traffic to other websites ■ Communications that drive the most traffic to a website ■ Most popular pages and content ■ Conversion of leads into customers	This type of analysis requires signing up for a service: it is free or premium in Google Analytics. Websites have to be 'tagged' so that data can be collected specific to each one. Raw data will have to be evaluated in light of goals and KPIs, such as: Goal: increase both the number of visitors to the site and the conversion (i.e., more visitors become event attendees)
Social media analysis: Analysis should target at least the following: ■ Textual data (actual words, comments) ■ Network data (such as Facebook Friendship Network, and Twitter follow-following network) ■ Actions (such as likes, shares, views) ■ Hyperlinks used ■ Location of users ■ Search engines used	Many companies offer specialized services to analyze social media pertinent to your interests. Events are increasingly monitoring and attempting to manage social media content, such as: ■ React swiftly to satisfy all complaints and correct false or negative rumours ■ Encourage certain activities such as purchases, re-tweeting, liking

There are many online resources for these types of analysis, for example from Colorado State University (https://writing.colostate.edu/guides/guide.cfm?guideid=61) for content analysis. Most website and social-media analysis sites are commercial in nature.

5.4.1 Checklists

An evaluator's toolbox is not complete without a full range of checklists. They are often where event evaluation begins, because checklists are so useful at the planning and operational stages and they lead directly to determination of completeness or deviation from specifications, and then to evaluation of what went wrong or could be done better.

Visit this site for advice on the uses of evaluation checklists and how to develop them: https://wmich.edu/evaluation/checklists. At this site Scriven explains different types of checklist (it's a downloadable PDF).

Figure 5.2: The Evaluator's Toolbox: Checklists

Purpose: checklists are valuable during the planning stage, process and summative evaluations; they can easily be combined with other methods, such as experience observation and photography.

Types and sample applications (adapted from Scriven)

1: Laundry list: when items on the list are completed or inspected, the box is ticked (e.g. a list of tasks for staff and volunteers)

2: Sequential checklist: do or inspect things in this order (e.g., the sequence of planned events, as in staging a parade)

3: Iterative checklist: do or confirm compliance more than once (e.g., a precise description of how the venue should be organised, such as the arrangement of tables and chairs, the décor, the access and egress routes, the lighting, at different times)

4: Diagnostic checklist: look for these signs or problems (e.g., for recycling check that bins and signs are in place; check to see that guests are using them properly; check that staff remove material according to schedule; note littering and environmental threats such as rain and wind; diagnosing potential risks, as in crowd behaviour)

5: Criteria of merit checklist: judge according to these criteria (e.g., criteria for awarding prizes and trophies).

Some Sources:

- https://wmich.edu/evaluation/checklists
- APEX Event Specifications Guide Template by the Convention Industry Council
- w ww.conventionindustry.org

William O'Toole (2011) in *Events Feasibility and Development* provides a series of checklists on: Queuing, VIPs, Tickets, Talent, Media, Exhibitors, 'on the day', transport, brochures, site, venue, promotion.

The Megan Jones book *Sustainable Event Management: A Practical Guide*, 3rd. ed. (2018) contains many checklists pertaining to going green and implementing sustainable practices.

Research Example: Getz, D., M. O'Neil and J. Carlsen, 2001. Service Quality Evaluation at Events Through Service Mapping. *Journal of Travel Research*, **39** (4), 380-390.

The authors conducted a systematic evaluation of a surfing event. Participant observation was combined with visitor surveys and a checklist used by a team of nine persons for observations of the site and visitors. Photos and videotaping were undertaken to provide a permanent record and to assist in the final analysis. Checklists were provided to all nine observers to directly record information of several types. Within specified areas at three preset times on each of Saturday and Sunday, observers counted the audience; estimated age, gender, and group characteristics; and made notes on crowd behavior and signs of impacts such as litter.

5.4.2 Case studies

Rarely used for evaluation purposes, this type of research can contribute to theory and provide comparisons that might help identify and solve problems. The research note provides an example from an event that was terminated, stressing the emotional attachment people had formed.

Otteman, T. & Janes, P. (2014). It is time? Ending a long-term event. *Event Management*, **18**, 369–376.

Abstract: This case study identifies strategies for ending long-term, cause-related events and provides techniques to manage loss of legacy and emotional attachment for participants. Participants from a 15-year charity golf event were studied before and after the final offering of the event. Questions included understanding why current and past participants decided to participate, the level of emotional attachment participants experienced with the event, and feelings regarding the termination of the event. Participants took part in the event because of the cause, to support the family organising the tournament, and because of the event's quality. Golfers were emotionally connected to the event and over half were not emotionally ready for the event to end.

5.5 Planning an evaluation

Stufflebeam provided a checklist for evaluation design that specifies the main evaluation project stages itemized below. (source: https://wmich.edu/sites/default/files/attachments/u350/2014/evaldesign.pdf)

5.5.1 The main evaluation project stages

1 *Focussing:* The first stage should make the following points explicit:
   - Purpose and goals (formative? process? summative?)
   - Ultimate uses – by whom?
   - Stakeholders who need to be consulted or advised
   - Scoping of the problem and what the evaluation requires; define the KEQ (see below)
   - Feasibility of the project, including resources committed and timeline
   - Consideration of any potential harmful impacts of the evaluation process or outcomes
   - Determination of the evaluation model and methods to be used. Is there underlying theory, or can a logic model be developed?

2 *Collecting information:* implementing the methodology, methods, and data collection

3 *Organising information:* database formation; security of data; access to data

4 *Analysing information:* qualitative and quantitative; interpretive

5 *Reporting:* related to intended uses of the evaluation

KEQ: Key Evaluation Question(s)

Identifying and agreeing upon KEQs will set direction and priorities for evaluations.

This entails defining the scope of the evaluation. Keeping it simple and focussed is often the best design. The KEQ will likely be determined by the purpose and the use to which the results will be put.

KEQ examples:

♦ Were our customers satisfied? (Context: the CEO needs data when reporting to the board, in two-weeks time)

♦ Did the event generate sufficient revenue for charity?

♦ Did we attain our goal of zero accidents/injuries? If not, why?

Monitoring or tracking the evaluation project

For complex and time-consuming evaluations activity tracking or monitoring tools are needed, including the critical path for getting the project finished. Advice on evaluation projects, including budgets and tracking is provided in the online document *Project Evaluation Guide For Nonprofit Organisations: Fundamental Methods and Steps For Conducting Project Evaluation* by Fataneh Theh and published by Imagine Canada (2006).

Contents of an evaluation report

♦ **Executive summary:** short summary of the evaluation process, results and key recommendations.

♦ **Introduction**: the background and the purposes of the evaluation; state key evaluation questions; explain if it is to solve problems, aid in decision-making, or if event/policy/programme worthiness is to be determined (i.e., the intended uses).

♦ **Evaluation methods and tools**: the evaluation plan, methods and measures used; append key instruments such as surveys; discuss adequacy of methods, any data gaps or possible reliability and validity issues.

♦ **Summary of results**: data and qualitative and quantitative analysis (not interpreted).

♦ **Interpretation of results:** readers need to know if interpretation is up to them, or has been made by specific people (the evaluators or stakeholders?); is there any reason for thinking bias has entered the interpretation? explain any uncertainties or inadequacies.

♦ **Conclusions**: show the logic of how conclusions were made; were the evaluation project objectives met? recommendations for action related to the objectives, for future evaluations or strategic planning.

5.5.2 Evaluation models

Figure 5.3 summarizes this discussion. The 'evaluation models' presented here range from simple to very complex, and represent options for event and tourism evaluators. They can be combined, just as qualitative and quantitative methods can be.

Figure 5.3: The Evaluator's Toolbox: Evaluation models and applications

	Important considerations
Deviation from standards or specifications The evaluator measures deviations and tries to determine why they happen and what can or should be done about them	This is one of the most basic and common forms of evaluation and absolutely necessary for events. See the discussion of checklists and performance standards in HR.
Comparisons: Case study, benchmarking A case study is one method, the intent being to study something in detail and determine if that sheds light on the real object of the evaluation. Case studies of evaluations can be beneficial. Benchmarking is a special case of comparison, requiring cooperation from the event or destination to be studied, then evaluation of exactly how they managed to solve a problem or, in broader scope, achieve success.	Comparison of standardized evaluations and impact assessments is one aim of collaboration, either among events or cities/destinations.
Time Series Evaluators will seldom have the luxury of extending a project years into the future to see what happens, but they can look back in time. The purpose is to identify trends and changes that can be attributed to events or tourism. This can be combined with comparisons.	Time-series analysis has been refined for the purpose of explaining and predicting tourism flows. Longitudinal research will be necessary for detecting long-term and cumulative impacts.
Quasi and field experiments Some kind of comparison group has to be found to provide evidence of cause and effect, but full controls are not possible.	Rarely used in the events and tourism fields. See Levy (2010) for an example
Experiments ■ Control groups are needed when cause and effect are to be determined. A caveat: providing proof in one situation does not in any way indicate that the same results will be obtained elsewhere.	True experiments are not generally relevant for events and tourism. Evaluators must obtain appropriate evidence of different kinds in order to make a compelling case.
Theory and logic models Theory based models start with a prediction based on theory, then seek confirmation. Logic models are similar but lack underlying predictive theory – the evaluator starts with the goals and sets out to determine if they were met, and how; logic models can also be based on experience	Discussed and illustrated in the next section.

Ethnographic; participant observation The rationale of ethnographic methods is that immersion in the problem, as in participating in a sport event or as an event volunteer, generates insights that cannot be obtained in any other way.	Examples are given in this book. Participation and systematic observation combined are powerful evaluation methods, but open to criticism of being biased.
Exploratory Evaluators might start by collecting data or opinions, even stories, then sort it out later either as evidence or to formulate a more structured evaluation model.	Researchers and evaluators often start with exploratory research and qualitative methods such as interviews, then, with new insights, proceed to quantitative data collection and analysis.
Expert judging Panels of experts often judge artistic performance, but who picks them? Judges are also found in all sports, as referees and officials who certify the outcome of competitions. Judging can be part of event and organisational certification, as in meeting green or sustainable standards.	Judging is discussed in Chapter 13 in the context of the arts.
Participatory/emancipatory How all stakeholder 'voices' are obtained, and conclusions drawn, can be a big challenge.	Stakeholder input to event planning and feedback as part of evaluation is always important. The participatory approach fits with interpretive or emancipatory paradigms, but there is no reason why any method cannot be employed.

5.6 Logic models

The logic for predicting outcomes has to come from theory, experience, or logical analysis of how one's actions cause change.

The 'logic model' is a tool for programme planners and evaluators, and is also useful in the context of project management where a final accounting will be required. Although a theory enabling prediction might not exist to guide planners and evaluators, they can still describe what they hope to accomplish (i.e., their goals), what it will take to achieve goals (inputs and activities) and what they will measure (such as key performance indictors, or feedback from stakeholders). Experience and research/evaluation leads to propositions about what can or should happen as a consequence of events, and that is theory building.

Figure 5.4 describes the steps in forming a logic model, and provides a hypothetical example. For more detail visit this site:

http://www.betterevaluation.org/resources/guids/results_chain/logic_models

Figure 5.4: The Evaluator's Toolbox: Logic models

Steps in forming logic models	Example
Step 1: Situation & needs analysis ■ Stakeholder engagement ■ Needs and priorities determined ■ Goals set The 'logic' of the plan has to be carefully articulated. What exactly will the event do to generate the desired outcomes? Is this logic based on theory or past experience? Unintended outcomes and externalities should also be considered.	Based on wide input from stakeholders three key goals for a new festival are formulated. Goal 1: foster community development by: engaging residents as organisers, volunteers, suppliers and performers; increased inter-organisational networking and collaboration Goal 2: Raise money for local projects Goal 3: Attract tourists and generate new income during an off-peak period; leverage the event to benefit local businesses
Step 2: Inputs ■ Who is investing? ■ Money, labour, information, equipment, supplies ■ Schedule and critical path developed ■ Action plan developed The needed inputs are derived from specifying the nature of the event (e.g., its costs, logistics, timing) and how it will be evaluated.	■ Social & leisure services provide grants and venues ■ Tourism covers market research and advertising ■ Community groups provide volunteers and services ■ A volunteer recruitment campaign is launched by the city ■ Local businesses are asked to make in-kind contributions ■ City staff, consultants and local residents plan the event as action research
Step 3: Actions and engagement (transforming processes) Both the event and the overall project are transforming processes. The intended outcomes have to be logically linked to actions taken to create and evaluate the event, and to the nature of the event itself. It is not adequate to assume that an event will automatically generate the desired benefits, nor is 'stakeholder satisfaction' an adequate sole indicator of success.	The project will involve transforming processes: ■ Recruitment and training of staff and volunteers ■ Assisting organisations to plan, collaborate, produce an event and raise money ■ Evaluation results will be transferred as knowledge to aid future planning The event will involve: ■ Free cultural performances, recreational activities, food and beverages and unique social experiences for visitors and participants will bring people together in sharing and celebration (each of these processes requires additional detail) ■ Special packages for tourists will provide additional value-for-money experiences

Step 4: Outputs	Goal attainment as measured by KPIs.
The evaluator first has to be able to provide convincing evidence that goals were achieved, as measured by pre- established KPIs (this demonstrates 'merit'). The 'worth' of the event (and therefore its future) will be established by stakeholders considering additional criteria such as stakeholder satisfaction, the nature of unintended outcomes, alternatives (or 'opportunity costs'), and how the event fits with event-tourism and social/cultural portfolios of different city and tourism agencies.	Samples: ▪ Knowledge gained (e.g. Recruit and train 100 volunteers) ▪ Generate x amount of money for community groups ▪ Foster improved city-community relations as measured by stakeholder feedback-100% volunteer satisfaction ▪ 80% Resident support (from a survey on use, attitudes and perceived impacts) ▪ Generate 500 local hotel bed nights during the off-peak ▪ 100% Positive feedback from industry partners – estimate of direct economic contribution matches or exceeds forecast evaluation feedback

The first two stages in the logic model are iterative, with purpose, goals and KPIs being formulated and revised as planning progresses and resources are committed. The planned actions are both the event and the overall project, both of which are (in combination) transforming processes.

Logic models can be graphic (see Figure 5.5), tabular or even verbal, as long as there is a clear, logical path stipulated from setting goals to evaluating expected outcomes. In this example a city works with community groups to create and produce a new cultural festival with the purpose of economic and social development in a disadvantaged area. Evaluation is built into the entire project so that it can be determined if the intervention works as planned, and how to improve the event.

It would be rare for an event to expect to generate permanent or long-term impacts, but that is a reasonable goal for a portfolio of events or event-tourism in general, and perhaps for some mega-events accompanied by massive investment. Special concerns for event tourism are indicated along the bottom of the model, with economic and community development being the desired impacts. Cumulative, long-term changes have to be demonstrated.

Figure 5.5: Logic model illustrated

**Logic model for goal-attainment evaluation:
Single event & event portfolios**

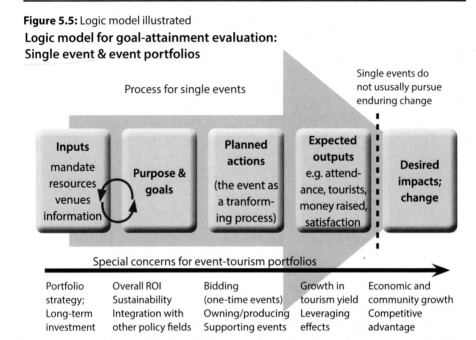

Recommended additional readings and sources

The Convention Industry Council: APEX Event Specifications Guide Template
    (www.conventionindustry.org)

Sustainable Measures (http://www.sustainablemeasures.com/node/92)

The Evaluation Center, Western Michigan University (https://wmich.edu/
    evaluation)

Better Evaluation (http://www.betterevaluation.org/resources/guids/
    results_chain/logic_models)

*Project Evaluation Guide For Nonprofit Organizations: Fundamental Methods and Steps
    For Conducting Project Evaluation* by Fataneh Theh and published by Imagine
    Canada (2006).

6 Establishing the Evaluation System

6.1 Introduction

This chapter provides the concepts necessary for establishing a permanent, comprehensive evaluation system. The recommended system is a goal-attainment model that ties in directly with strategic planning and enables continuous improvement. The essential ingredients are goals, key performance indicators, and a toolbox of methods. There are limitations to this approach, so we discuss 'tunnel vision' and how to prevent it.

These are the aims of a comprehensive system for event and event-tourism evaluation:

♦ Be a permanent, systematic and well integrated part of the organisation.

♦ Help implement a learning organisation and contribute to continuous improvement, innovation, and adaptation.

♦ Provide essential data and feedback within event/tourism planning and management.

♦ Reflect all stakeholder concerns and diverse values related to the economic, environmental, social and cultural dimensions of events and tourism.

♦ Reflect both extrinsic and intrinsic approaches to evaluation.

◆ Derive from, reinforce and assist in the formation of strategy.

◆ Employ goal-attainment and utilize key performance indicators.

◆ Be able to identify unexpected, negative and external outcomes.

◆ Apply methods and measures appropriate to wide-ranging issues.

◆ Provide sound and actionable evidence for making decisions, solving problems, and establishing merit and worth.

6.2 The learning organisation

Peter Senge popularized the concept of the learning organisation through his 1990 book *The Fifth Discipline*. According to Senge (1990:3) learning organisations are:

> *"… organisations where people continually expand their capacity to create the results they truly desire, where new and expansive patterns of thinking are nurtured, where collective aspiration is set free, and where people are continually learning to see the whole together."*

Senge believed that only flexible, adaptive and productive organisations will excel. There is a competitive advantage for an organisation whose workforce can learn more quickly than other organisations. The organisation must provide an environment, or culture, in which reflection and engagement are encouraged.

Senge articulated five basic 'disciplines' required for learning organisations.

◆ The first is *systems thinking*, viewing the organisation as a whole in relation to its environment – more on this follows.

◆ The second discipline is *personal mastery*, being the commitment by individuals to the process of learning, and from this mechanisms must be established to ensure the entire organisation learns.

◆ *Mental models* are the assumptions held by individuals and organisations, and they must be challenged. Organisational culture, embodying values, mental models and theories about how things should be done, is often a reflection of founders' visions and is resistant to change. But a learning organisation has to foster an open culture, meaning that evaluation has to lead to changes.

◆ The fourth discipline is *shared vision*, which can motivate staff to evaluate and learn. Senge argued that flat, decentralized organisational structures are best for this, not one in which a vision is imposed top-down. Vision leads to goals.

◆ Fifth is *team learning* and this discipline seems especially relevant in event management. Teams must be open to other teams, and accumulating knowledge must inform organisational learning. Knowledge management systems have to be put in place, and this includes evaluation.

6.2.1 Organisational culture

The learning organisation introduces a related concept, that of *organisational culture*. Here is a definition:

"The values and behaviors that contribute to the unique social and psychological environment of an organisation. Organisational culture includes an organisation's expectations, experiences, philosophy, and values that hold it together, and is expressed in its self-image, inner workings, interactions with the outside world, and future expectations. It is based on shared attitudes, beliefs, customs, and written and unwritten rules that have been developed over time and are considered valid."

Source: http://www.businessdictionary.com/definition/ organisational-culture.html

Organisational cultures are unique and can be difficult to change. Why might evaluation be resisted? Some events are essentially amateurish (and this is not the same as being incompetent) and the leaders or volunteers want to avoid bureaucracy, complications, and extra work; they are happy doing things in the same way and will resist change in general. Even in professionally-managed organisations the dominant culture might be one of "this is how we do things" or "we always did it this way and it's good enough". In these contexts, leadership is the issue. Finally, and all too common, a lack of resources (money, people, time) is a source of resistance to change in general and evaluation in particular.

6.3 The triple-bottom-line and the balanced scorecard

These two concepts have found a place in management theory and ethics, and both provide a foundation for our recommended event evaluation system.

6.3.1 Triple-bottom-line

According to Wikipedia:

"Triple bottom line (or otherwise noted as TBL or 3BL) is an accounting framework with three parts: social, environmental (or ecological) and financial. Many organisations have adopted the TBL framework to evaluate their performance in a broader perspective to create greater business value. The term was coined by John Elkington in 1994."

TBL – what does it mean to evaluators? First, it is a philosophy, not a method or system. It encourages broader, longer-term planning and accountability but does not fully encompass principles of steady-state sustainability. I use TBL as a short form when talking about comprehensive impact assessment and sustainable development, and it is also an introduction to the balanced scorecard.

Incommensurability has been a major limitation of TBL. It means the lack of comparable measures for economic (almost always monetary), social/cultural and environmental impacts or performance. The goal attainment model called Event

Compass overcomes this limitation by emphasizing goal attainment, KPIs and continuous improvement.

6.3.2 Balanced scorecard

Attributed mostly to Kaplan and Norton (1992), this integrated management system was designed to go beyond the short-termed thinking of most companies, in which financial performance and profits dominated. More recently it has been adapted to include sustainability, stakeholder and CSR perspectives on the organisation.

Kaplan and Norton stressed that "information age companies" have to be guided through investment in customers, suppliers, processes, technology and innovation.

The original model of the balanced scorecard features four dimensions labelled "financial, customer, internal process, and learning and growth". For each of these, objectives are to be formulated, plus key performance measures, action plans and of course evaluation plus feedback. Software is now readily available for implementing the scorecard system and ensuring that everyone in the organisation has access to the plan and the metrics – but it is not necessarily suitable for events and tourism.

For event and tourism organisations some important modifications can be made, depending on their profit or service orientations. The financial dimension of the scorecard has sometimes been renamed 'stewardship', reflecting the ideology that the resources are to be used for public good, and the environment must be respected by the organisation – thereby reflecting a sustainability approach. My illustration, Figure 6.1, therefore subsumes stewardship under sustainability.

The focus on customers can be expanded to include all stakeholders, recognizing social responsibility principles and the principle that organisations will perform better when stakeholder interests (rather than just shareholders) are part of the strategy.

"Internal process" can be expanded to "internal or transforming processes" which can include producing an event or managing an event portfolio. But I have indicated evaluation and learning and continuous improvement as the main elements.

I have replaced "learning and growth" with " organisational culture", reflecting the principles of the learning organisation and systems thinking. It includes capacity building for learning, growth, and adaptability. Innovation fits here, as an evaluation system is necessary for learning and continuous improvement.

In the center of the diagram is the planning process, which is always cyclical. "Mandate" relates to the type of organisation (e.g. profit or service oriented), and "vision" indicates the desired future state. Although we are focussed on evaluation in this book, it is really part of the planning cycle and provides feedback for formulating and revising strategy, goals and indicators.

Figure 6.1: Modified balanced scorecard concept for event management and event tourism (adapted from Kaplan and Norton, 1992)

6.3.3 Evolution of the scorecard

The first generation scorecards in the 1990s focused on metrics and control, but did little to advance strategy and innovation. In second generation scorecards the emphasis was placed on key performance indicators that are believed to drive growth or success. So-called third generation approaches stress 'strategy mapping' and/or 'destination statements'. A strategy map shows graphically the vision or 'destination statement' (see below for examples) and how the organisation gets there by reference to the four main elements of the scorecard.

Phil Jones (2011), in the book *Strategy Mapping for Learning Organisations*, established a fourth-generation approach, with the emphasis on learning.

Generic strategy map for event tourism

There are unlimited possibilities for the design and contents of a strategy map – the internet is full of examples. The logic starts with the main elements of a balanced scorecard, and these can be called 'enablers' as they are the foundation for achieving desired outcomes. A 'destination statement' sets the vision, which is of course linked to the organisation's mandate; statements of 'core values' may be included here.

Actions, perhaps expressed as an action plan with budgets and time lines, must be clearly linked to desired or expected outcomes, and be stated as value propositions. In the case of events there might be specific clients seeking an ROI, while tourism and event development agencies are generally creating triple-bottom-line value primarily for residents, but also for other stakeholders such as private businesses. Key performance indicators are included here, as these are the measures of value. Evaluation is one of the essential internal processes.

Figure 6.2: Generic strategy map structure

Destination statement: mandate, vision, core values

Outcomes/impacts: with key performance indicators
Value: to be created for residents and other stakeholders
– economic, ecological, built environment, social, cultural

Action plan: the transforming processes that create value, each linked to desired outcomes

Enablers: organisational culture (learning & growth); internal processes; customers/stakeholders; finances/stewardship/sustainability

6.3.4 Elements of balanced scorecards and strategy mapping

In some respects the strategy map is similar to logic models.

Vision: sometimes refereed to as a 'destination statement', or where the organisation wants to be in five or ten years' time; this will have to be more precise than "we want to be the biggest or best", as that level of ambiguity cannot possibly guide strategy to action and evaluation.

Relevant metrics: what we evaluate and measure has to be linked clearly to implementing the strategy and realizing the vision.

Causality: the event has to be confident (i.e., it makes predictions) that certain actions will achieve desired outcomes; these can be based on theory and reflected in strategy maps or logic models.

Ownership and buy-in: leaders have to ensure the strategy is followed, performance is evaluated, and staff/volunteers know what is expected; the potential downside is that everyone becomes a slave to the system and innovation is reduced, otherwise implementing the vision and strategy makes the organisation inflexible.

Adaptability: Evaluators have a role that goes beyond metrics, they become an essential part of learning, and learning leads to adaptation – often requiring changes in the strategy or vision.

Implementing the system

Below is a planning sequence for implementing the balanced scorecard or any other evaluation system. Users can adapt it to their situation, as profit-driven organisations will have different priorities than government agencies and not-for-profits. I have tried to make this as inclusive as possible, but it does mostly reflect a service rather than a profit orientation.

Step 1: Prepare a vision statement that reflects your mission or mandate

This sets the stage for strategy and actions. Consider all your stakeholders, especially target groups or clients, residents, and suppliers or co-producers. Incorporate social responsibility and sustainability principles. Remember that this vision has to be translated into strategy and action plans, with appropriate objectives and/or performance indicators. Organisational culture might become an impediment to change, so consider how the system can be implemented, if at all.

Step 2: Prepare a strategy plan for customers/clients/target groups and other stakeholders

How does the event give value or create public good? Is it simply through entertainment, or is the event itself intended to be an agent of change? Is it an integral part of a managed portfolio? How important, relative to each other, are the potential economic and social/cultural benefits? Will the event create clear benefits, and are the costs worth it? What harm or environmental damage might occur, and can it be prevented and/or ameliorated?

The strategy plan for customers and other stakeholders should indicate exactly how benefits will be generated, and for whom. This gets translated into actions and performance criteria.

Step 3: Prepare a strategy plan for sustainability (financial viability/economics, greening, stewardship, social responsibility, community engagement)

Sustainability requires continued financial viability, so a strategy for acquiring adequate resources is needed. This should be complemented by efficiency improvements, reduced resource dependency, and committed support from critical stakeholders like local government and corporate sponsors. Greening and environmental standards should be met, whereas social responsibility requires engagement with the community and other legitimate stakeholders.

Step 4: Prepare a strategy plan for internal or transformational processes

This will have to be broken down into functional areas, with particular attention to human resources. As many events are dependent on volunteers, their commitment to the system has to be part of the strategy. The principle of 'cascading' applies here. The mandate/mission and the vision have to be communicated and accepted throughout the organisation and shared with key stakeholders, like a waterfall. Consistency of implementation at all levels, from the board of directors down to the smallest or weakest link, might be difficult to achieve. Incentives or rewards might be required to ensure buy-in at all levels. Workers and stakehold-ers need to understand how their efforts contribute to the strategy. This is often called the 'alignment' of goals and actions with strategy and vision.

Step 5: Prepare a strategy for changing organisational culture (including learning and growth, adaptability, evaluation, and continuous improvement)

To be a 'learning organisation' requires an evaluation system tied to mandate, vision and strategy. Continuous improvement is to be enabled, especially when it comes to social responsibility and environmental sustainability. Training and professional development for staff, volunteers and leaders are part of this process. An efficient information management system, part of overall knowledge manage-ment, is a necessity and this might include software designed specifically for the scorecard system.

Other enablers have to be included, especially resources and public/political support. Commitment from various stakeholders is often an essential capacity builder. And consider the various forms of 'capital' that have to be invested to produce an event and achieve goals, including human, financial, knowledge, and social (i.e., networks and relationships).

Step 6: Write objectives / set targets

Objectives are usually statements defining targets or necessary outcomes, such as "each year we will generate at least 5,000 in surplus revenue". It is obvious if you meet the target or not. But they could be non-quantifiable statements of intent, each one linked to a broad goal and an event broader strategy. Consider this hierarchy:

♦ *Strategy*: continuous improvement of the event experience in order to ensure financial viability

♦ *Goal*: maximise customer enjoyment through high-quality entertainment

♦ *Quantifiable objective*: each year, obtain at least 80% customer satisfaction

♦ *Qualitative objective*: each year, improve the quality of performance

The quantifiable metric is clear, being satisfaction, but the qualitative requires some thought. How do you judge quality performance?

Step 7: Select metrics / KPIs

Measuring customer satisfaction is one of the most common metrics employed in event evaluation, obtained usually through on-site or follow-up surveys. An indirect measure could be used as well, such as observing behaviour (are guests attentive? distracted? staying longer?). Importance-Performance measures yield more information. Once the metrics are known, key performance indicators can be set. However, it is often going to be an iterative process, working out what you want to measure and determining if it is practical.

Step 8: Formulate cascading action plans; set budgets

'Cascading action plans' means that you start with a big, general strategy, then create more and more specific action plans to achieve your goals – each one is more detailed or refined than the last. Action plans require decisions on who is responsible, and what resources they will have to do the job.

Step 9: Implement evaluation methods; monitoring

Monitoring, or ongoing data collection and maintenance of an information system, is a necessary foundation for evaluation. If the data are not readily available the evaluator has to get it.

Step 10: Utilize evaluation/metrics for continuous improvement

The metrics for implementing a balanced scorecard are context-specific. For events, continuous improvement can mean quite different things, and tourism adds yet another dimension. The implication is that TBL and scorecards – any evaluation system in fact – has to be customized for the organisation.

Study questions

1   Describe how the "learning organisation" depends upon evaluation, and how organisational culture might be an impediment to establishing a comprehensive evaluation system.

2   Are Triple Bottom Line and Balanced Scorecard models the same? Explain how an event or tourism organisation can incorporate these models into its culture and strategic planning.

3   Prepare a strategy map for an event or tourism organisation and specify in detail the evaluation components.

Recommended additional readings and sources

Jones, P. (2011). *Strategy Mapping for Learning Organizations.* Farnham, England: Gower.

Kaplan, R.S. & Norton, D.P. (1992). The balanced scorecard – Measures that drive performance. *Harvard Business Review* (January–February), 71–79.

Senge, P. (1990). *The Fifth Discipline: The Art & Practice of The Learning Organization.* New York: Century Business, Doubleday. (revised, 2006)

7 Goals and Goal Attainment

Learning objectives

1 Understand the logic and limitations of a goal-attainment approach to evaluation.

2 Be able to discuss the advantages and disadvantages of goal-free evaluation.

3 Know the meaning of 'externalities' and how evaluators can deal with them.

4 Be able to develop service specifications (i.e., The 'service blueprint') from a detailed work plan.

5 Understand the importance of task analysis and work clusters, as they relate to teamwork and evaluation.

6 Learn goal attainment and evaluation lessons from the evaluation systems called the Event Compass.

7 Be able to use an evaluation system for continuous improvement.

8 Understand the importance of encouraging the use of standard methods and measures so that a database can be created for comparisons, benchmarking and meta-analysis.

7.1 Introduction

For systematic evaluation and strategic planning, and for complex evaluation problems, the approach recommended in this book, and reflected in the Event Compass, is a goal-attainment model. So we need to define some terms here.

Goal: desired result or outcome; intended end-point

Long-term goals are associated with vision and strategy, while short-term goals pertain to the kind of outputs that are more easily and quickly attainable, such as the target attendance and revenue to be raised for an event. Long-term goals might relate in general to achieving the vision or sustaining success, but can also specify desired impacts (or outcomes) that imply changes in society or the economy. In a tourism context long-term goals might be tied to the management of portfolios of events and their desired/predicted cumulative impacts.

One event cannot usually be expected to have outcome/impact goals that imply long-term, permanent changes in systems. Perhaps mega-events can aim that high, but system change is more in the realm of event portfolios and tourism in general, being permanent and major components of city and destination strategies.

Goals are expressed in general terms and usually require the accompaniment of performance measures. These can be called *objectives*, the attainment of which can be measured. The terms 'goal' and 'objective' are technically synonymous and therefore confusion can result, so in this book we use indicators and KPIs instead of 'measureable objectives'.

7.2 Goal-free evaluation

What if an event or tourism causes changes or impacts that are beyond the scope of its goals? Unanticipated effects, and 'externalities' are common occurrences, so if the evaluator only looks at goal attainment some problems might be missed.

> *Externality*: *an impact that occurs as a consequence of events or tourism, the cost of which is borne by others (i.e., externalities are not part of the event's accounts).*

There are many examples, ranging from pollution (who cleans up if water is contaminated? what long-term impact does the carbon emitted from event tourism cause?) to social and cultural impacts such as inflation, displacement of the poor from affordable housing or crime and amenity loss. These things are seldom if ever incorporated into the planning and evaluation of events, and that represents a major problem for achieving sustainability goals.

In goal-free evaluation (attributed to Scriven, 1991b), a systems approach is taken by external, impartial evaluators. They do not start with the stated goals of the organisation; they start with identification of what was done and proceed to identify the outputs and, if possible, the longer term outcomes or impacts. Actual costs and benefits to stakeholders are considered.

This approach can uncover externalities and generate recommendations for how to deal with them. It can also avoid a potential pitfall of goal-attainment models: if you look for something, you will find it! So if the goal is to create a positive destination image through event tourism, an evaluation might go to great lengths to find evidence of success. The feedback from goal-free evaluation can inform strategy and lead to a better alignment of strategy, goals and actual effects.

Goal-free evaluation is not easy to do and will require experts, time and money to do properly, hence it is not all that common. That is why it is best thought of as a mind-set, or guiding principle when evaluations are done. The evaluator using a goal-attainment model should not fall into the trap of 'tunnel vision', being a narrow focus on goals, to the exclusion of searching for side effects or externalities.

How is that to be done? Through the participation of 'downstream' stakeholders, including residents. They will see things differently and inform a more complete evaluation. 'Upstream stakeholders' are the ones sponsoring the event or tourism and their input will be part of the evaluator's mandate, however they can be biased towards producing a favourable evaluation. The downstream stakeholders are the ones actually impacted by an event and by tourism.

7.2.1   Overcoming tunnel vision

To avoid tunnel vision the evaluator must think systematically and ask questions that go well beyond "did we attain our goals?" More importantly, the organisation's evaluation system has to reflect TBL and balanced scorecard thinking, as embodied in the Event Compass. Here is a diagram to keep in mind.

Figure 7.1: Overcoming tunnel vision

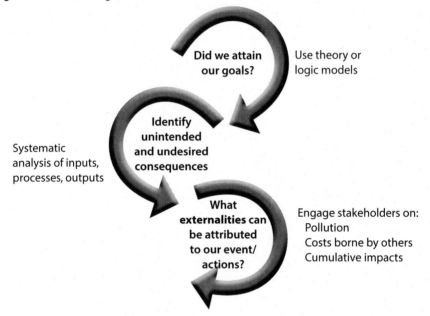

7.3   Task analysis and the work plan

If you know in advance what exactly is to be done by everyone involved in the event, in the form of a complete work plan, then evaluation becomes much simpler. Any deviation from the work plan becomes an issue to examine: why did it happen? was it important? should we do things differently? Looking back, in post-event evaluation, the work plan will provide clues about the causes of problems. For example, if customers were dissatisfied by having to wait a long time to enter a facility, was that due to the required staff numbers not being present on time (as planned) or to another, unanticipated reason?

The work plan is all too often not specified, just as service specifications (the blueprint) are often unwritten, and that leads to problems. On the other hand, the detail required is potentially enormous, and therefore it is wise to use project management software.

Tasks and interdependencies among tasks have to be identified, for all programmes and facilities, and for all workers. Later, a critical path analysis will determine the sequencing of these tasks. O'Toole (2011) provided worksheets for related analyses, and task analysis was also covered in an earlier book (O'Toole and Mikolaitis, 2002).

A work plan can proceed from two starting points:

♦ An a priori description of the event, where its detailed elements are known in advance (for example, a sport event or function that has a standard structure); a good place to start might be with the venue(s), or perhaps a description of each activity or programme, and these can be thought of as work clusters. Sequencing them is important.

♦ A statement of goals and objectives leading to development of the final structure of the event (for example, planning a celebration with a known theme but yet-to-be-developed programme and setting)

Take logistics as an example. There will be teams of staff and volunteers assigned to different logistical needs including the movement of equipment, people movement, and food and beverage services. For the task "entrance to the venue" there are a number of challenges: policing, parking, ticketing and handling cash, giving directions and information, and assisting those in need. All the details for these tasks feed directly into the service blueprint, and it also requires detailed consideration of how the guest/customer will experience the event. Where might there be critical incidents that affect satisfaction, such as long waiting times or poor signage? How many workers are needed to ensure a smooth flow? What are the safety hazards? Do we need police outside and inside?

For every task or work cluster a performance standard can be specified, although this will lead to a rather large list. An alternative is to stress teamwork and prepare somewhat more general specifications for work clusters – in this case 'entrance to the venue').

7.4 Case study: The Event Compass

Every organisation needs its own permanent, comprehensive evaluation system. The Event Compass, described here in detail, is a model that can be adapted to many different circumstances. It was developed at Mid-Sweden University under the direction of Dr. Robert Pettersson with consulting input from Professor Donald Getz (Canada) and Dr. Steve Brown (Australia). Here are its main features:

♦ A comprehensive system designed especially for event evaluation

♦ Merges evaluation with strategic planning

♦ Embodies principles of systems thinking, triple-bottom-line, and the balanced scorecard

♦ Fosters continuous improvement

♦ Follows a goal attainment approach that eliminates the need for employing the same metrics across its dimensions

♦ Allows flexibility in setting and weighting goals

♦ Uses key performance indicators

♦ Potentially can be used in certifying events

♦ Can be adapted to venues and attractions or other services.

Its basic concepts can easily be adapted to widespread use by any type of event, incorporating goal-attainment along eight dimensions, each with a set of KPIs. The Compass embodies a TBL approach with KPIs for evaluating the event/organisation and its impacts.

7.4.1 Dimensions and sub-dimensions

Illustrated in Figure 7.2 are five main management dimensions: organisation, planning, marketing, risk and design. These do not delimit the full scope of what a given organisation or event might want to include – they are a starting point. As well, each dimension can be broken down into sub-dimensions with their own goals and KPIs. It is even possible to devote the entire Compass to one dimension, focusing, for example, on Risk or Marketing.

Figure 7.2: The Event Compass - Concept

Similarly, the three impact dimensions of economic, environmental, and social/cultural impacts (reflecting the standard TBL approach) are a starting point. I think cultural and social impacts deserve separate treatment, as does the built environment – separate from ecological systems. What matters most is that adoption of the Compass entails thinking systematically and developing a comprehensive evaluation system tied to strategic planning.

7.4.2 Options for comparative measurement

Within a TBL approach to impact assessment there is always the problem of comparing monetary units with non-monetary metrics. Economic impacts are almost always measured in terms of money, but environmental impacts include metrics like the carbon and ecological footprints.

Unless surrogate monetary measures are employed, the three dimensions of TBL cannot be directly compared. The article by Andersson, Armbrecht and Lundberg (2016) describes an approach employing use and non-use values and a monetary measure for the ecological footprint.

Research note

Tommy D. Andersson, John Armbrecht & Erik Lundberg (2016) Triple impact assessments of the 2013 European athletics indoor championship in Gothenburg, *Scandinavian Journal of Hospitality and Tourism*, **16**(2), 158-179.

ABSTRACT: This study answers the call for holistic assessments of events' sustainability through testing a model for measuring impacts of a sports tourism event from sustainability perspectives and in a common monetary metric. The aim is to achieve commensurability through integration of economic, sociocultural and environmental impacts. Concepts such as use- and non-use value, consumer surplus, direct economic impacts, ecological footprint analysis and shadow cost are applied to fulfil this aim. The model is tested on a three-day long European athletics indoor championship 2013 and the results demonstrate a possibility to produce a sustainability impact analysis in a uniform metric.

Measurement options for the event compass

When you want to compare all five management dimensions and all three impact dimensions, you either need the same metric (e.g., money) or another form of comparison. The 'radar graph' in Figure 7.3 uses a scale of 0-100, defining the degree to which goals have been obtained. Here are some options for the scale:

a) Use a scale of 0-100 with 0 meaning "nothing has been done" and 100 meaning "we have achieved all our goals in this dimension". Note that as 100% goal attainment is approached, the fundamental idea of continuous improvement comes into play – set higher goals! The total score is either a subjective evaluation of progress or, for more precision, a sum of all the goals for that dimension.

b) assign a 0-100 value to each KPI and use the sum these scores to generate the score for each goal; this is more precise than (a)

c) instead of a precise scale use a broader, more subjective system such as:

   D-no progress towards goal attainment

   C-some progress, but inadequate

   B-considerable progress has been made but more must be done

   A-full attainment of the goal / KPI

7.4.3 Priorities and weighting

Which of the eight dimensions is most important? In theory they are all important, but any one, or several, dimensions might have higher priority. That can be determined through a baseline evaluation by managers, external experts or a certifying body. The same goes for individual goals and KPIs. For example, an event might want to focus on environmental impacts and specifically the goal of reducing waste. This leads to giving a higher priority or *weight* to this goal and related KPIs such as "amount of food waste composted on site".

The weighting of metrics can be important. In a not-for-profit, service-oriented festival, for example, the social-cultural dimensions and its goals and KPIs might very well be considered twice as important as economic goals. The opposite might hold true for events produced or supported by tourism agencies. As for the management functions, the risk dimension (which can include financial risks as well as accidents and illness) might for some events or agencies be crucial, and therefore deserve a higher weight than design.

How is weighting reflecting in the comparison? If a 0-100 scale is used, any of the priority dimensions can subsequently be singled out for special attention – the scale itself does not have to change. Alternatively, the goals and KPIs can be made easier to achieve.

Another way to stress priority dimensions or goals is to single them out for a separate evaluation.

Figure 7.3 shows how the Compass can be used to measure goal-attainment progress in all eight dimensions by way of a 'radar graph'. Users can add dimensions and sub-dimensions.

Figure 7.3: Sample Event Compass radar graph

An example is for the "organisation" domain, and this is the subject of the very next chapter. Note that goals can be expressed in different ways, but it is normal to express them in terms of something to be achieved or completed. In this example the overall goals pertain to being a competent, enduring and successful event or event-tourism organisation, so the KPIs are measures of specific things that need to be done. This approach is also suitable for certification by an outside body, in which case the KPIs provide a checklist of items that have to be in place. This also follows the logic of the 'strategy map' described earlier.

Figure 7.4: The example of the organisational domain

Goals & sub goals	Key performance indicators	Data sources / methods
We will become an innovative, learning organisation.	■ Developed and communicated a clear vision for the organisation.	■ Official documents of the organisation.
■ We will develop a permanent, comprehensive evaluation system	■ Evaluation is integrated into all management functions and is completed for all events.	■ Interviews with owners, directors and managers
■ Our vision for ten years into the future is to be the most successful event in our area	■ Success to be judged by reference to increasing attendance and surplus revenue.	■ The organisation's internal accounts and audited financial statements
		■ Stakeholder feedback

7.4.4 Detailed description of the Event Compass

The following description is provided by the Event Compass team at Mid-Sweden University. They offer a number of services to assist events and organisations in adopting and utilizing the system.

"The Event Compass™ offers a range of research-based solutions that serve the interests of event organisers, event goers and host communities alike. The Event Compass process can be encapsulated by the three cornerstones Evaluation, Recommendation and Certification.

By evaluating event processes and impacts we form a profile of your event on which we can outline the most efficient line of action for you to achieve sustainable success and meet the demands of key stakeholders.

The *Baseline Evaluation* is geared towards bringing an event organisation up to the Event Compass standard through a set of well-tested indicators. The compulsory and point criteria are created around management processes. Once the standard has been achieved, an EC certification is granted to communicate industry excellence.

Further impact evaluations are offered in packages that are modeled to meet the needs of an event and its particular context. These impact evaluations are gauged through a benchmarking database and expert guidance is then provided to initiate a process of continual self-improvement on these important areas.

The Dimensions

The EC Dimensions are the building blocks of our event evaluation and consultancy. They are divided into five internal process dimensions and three external impact dimensions. The process dimensions consist of *Organisation, Planning, Marketing, Design* and *Risk*. In short they represent elements that should be a part of any successful and responsible event organisation.

Impact dimensions are concerned with the outputs of the event organisation. Outputs both in terms of the events performance held up against its own objectives but also its impacts on the host community, the event goers and the environment. The impact dimensions are therefore divided into the triple bottom line consisting of *Economic, Environmental* and *Socio-Cultural*.

The *Organisation* dimension covers the structure and general managerial mechanisms of the event firm. The organisation is the backbone and basic building block of the firm that influences the way in which all of the other internal dimensions are formed and run. In it we find functions that deal with the allocation of human resources, hierarchies, total quality management, the business model and daily operations amongst other areas. Evaluating this dimension involves checking the presence and correct use of key processes and competencies in the organisational sphere.

Planning implies strategic decision-making, often several years ahead. Long-term planning is something of a rarity amongst event organisers, and is therefore one of the key areas where our clients see the most significant improvements upon using our services. Strategic planning stems from the vision, objectives, philosophy and policy formulation of the firm and extends its influence over longer time periods. Implementing a strategy entails making changes to current operations with future goals in mind. An example would be using goal attainment to reach a zero CO_2 emission goal for an annual event over a 10-year period. For every event, the objective is to reduce emissions by 10% towards the final goal. The firm is thereby given the opportunity to gradually adapt and do so cost-effectively over this period. Other potential usages for strategic planning and goal setting are within product development. A strategy of this nature could focus on widening the range of events on offer in the firm's/destination's portfolio or expanding the size and contents of existing events.

Risk management is just as much a question of risk mitigation as it is one of having a set of mechanisms and SOPs in place when unexpected events do occur. It requires an inventory or risk assessment be made listing the types of risks an event might be subject to. A prioritization should then be made weighing the costs and benefits of addressing each risk factor. The Event Compass works with leading risk and crisis experts to guide organisers in this process.

Design: In event research, design is closely connected to the experience value of the event to the visitor. Good design in this sense implies starting off with the experience in mind, and forming the event with the interplay of its different components, around it. Conversely, bad design arises when an organiser takes a reductionist approach and focuses on layout in terms of its practical qualities.

In the interest of measurability, design in the Baseline Evaluation will focus on the aesthetic and functional elements of the product/event. Services available to event-goers, the activity content and the physical environment of the event are focal points of design. If marketing conveys the event experience and convinces people to attend, the design element is the final product that determines the visitor's experience and thus their satisfaction. The design element of an event organisation also has considerable influence on efficiencies and flows. Hence, operational costs and environmental impacts, for example, can be directly affected by efforts in this dimension.

The Marketing dimension is concerned with the specific processes that form the market value of the firm's brand and products as well as those that impact the accessibility of these products to the consumer. Some marketing functions handle strategic questions where competitor analysis, demand analysis (market research) and market positioning are in focus. The other purpose of marketing is to deal with operative stages such as projecting the brand's value on to the market, doing so using effective communication tools, finding the right communication channels to employ these tools through, minimizing gaps in expected and perceived service delivery (SERVQUAL) and following up this process through continual evaluation.

The *Economic dimension* handles all economic outputs/externalities of the event firm and the individual event. Values measured range from the direct economic impacts on the host community and the world to the more complex indirect impacts, both being of great interest to event researchers. In the case of the Baseline Evaluation, it is the organisational processes that influence these values that are scrutinized. Direct impacts include tangible values such as revenue in the form of tourism receipts and jobs generated by the event organisation itself. Indirect impacts are hotly debated and serve as one of the main arguments for the need of a research-based approach to event evaluation. These include measurements of catalytic and multiplier effects relevant to the greater region hosting an event.

The *Environmental dimension* might well represent one of the most polarizing topics in modern society. Stemming from the environmental movement of the 60s, it gained further legitimacy through the sustainability discourse of the 80s as solidified by the Brundtland commission. Commercial human activity and especially activity that involves significant numbers of people almost invariably has an adversarial relationship to the natural environment. Thus, the outputs that are evaluated in the environmental dimension principally consist of negative externalities. As a general rule, environmental indicators should display low values. Exceptions to this rule are the instances where outcomes are intangible and where instead inputs in e.g. education and conservation efforts might be the values to measure.

The *Social and Cultural dimensions* are grouped together in the Event Compass. The reasoning goes that cultural expressions are an inherent part of the social life of all communities. Part of this link can be found in physical cultural manifestations such as infrastructure, art exhibitions, performance art, theatre, music and so on. These are all represent tangible culture and they hold the inventory of a society's signs and symbols. Signs and symbols are in turn powerful indicators of the values of said society. For example, the story, language used and props of local stage play will reflect the political and social values of the community (read cultural context) it was created in. The other interface between the social and the cultural can be found in the identity of individuals and groups. Society is made up of an overlapping constellation of groups, all with their own cultural attributes that include the earlier mentioned signs and symbols, values, norms, customs and language. Beyond the biological/psychological factors that influence their behaviour, each individual is also a product of a unique combination of group identities. The group identities one can be influenced by include national and regional (geographic), demographic, hedonistic (i.e. hobbies), urban/rural and the list goes on. Event experiences are highly socio-cultural phenomena as they offer cultural capital to the consumers and an arena where they can share their interests. The value of this event experience and its potential cultural capital is gauged through the filter of the visitor's unique cultural lens. Events also contribute to the social life of host communities, enhancing the 'sense of place' and boosting community pride."

7.5 The toolbox and database

Researchers and evaluators need a toolbox of methods and measures that can be adapted to many purposes, plus a database for comparisons (i.e., benchmarking and meta analysis) to inform planning. Tools and data can be shared, so this is a job that might best be done by professional or event associations, cities and destination organisations. Figure 7.5 below illustrates important data sources to be used in event and event-tourism evaluation – in effect a list of key stakeholders. For each of these, standard methods and measures should be developed. Standardization is important for several reasons:

♦ Standard methods and measures facilitate valid comparisons, benchmarking and meta analysis.

♦ Standardization makes certification of events and organisations easier and more valid.

♦ Using approved, standard methods and measures generates trust and hopefully more political support (especially when it comes to impact assessment).

Figure 7.5: Sources of information, data required and methods

Sources of information	Data required, and methods
The organisation	Fully described in Chapters 8 and 9: documentation of all management systems and evaluations; compliance with standards
Staff and volunteers	Essential feedback through performance evaluations and other consultations on: effectiveness and efficiency of all management systems; satisfaction and commitment
Audiences/ visitors	Fully described in Chapter 10: data from visitor/attendee surveys and other market research

Partners, co-producers	Presumably they are directly involved in planning and decision-making. Obtain feedback on satisfaction, concerns and recommendations for improvement.
Clients	For corporate and association events, accountability is required yielding direct feedback on goal attainment, satisfaction, recommendations
Event owners or governing bodies	For sports in particular, full accountability is required, yielding data on the meeting of all specifications, satisfaction and recommendations
Residents and community groups	Periodic consultations and surveys in the community to yield data on: production of or support for event; attendance and participation in events; attitudes towards events and tourism; perception of impacts (positive and negative) and their importance; use and non-use values
Sponsors and grant givers	Accountability reports will be needed for sponsors and grant givers, and this will generate feedback on: the extent of, and commitment to supporting events; conditions for assistance; their goals; how they evaluate
Suppliers and local business	Suppliers to provide data on sales, logistical issues, compliance with policies (e.g., green practices), satisfaction and recommendations for improvement of relationships
	Periodic consultations with local businesses (tourism, hospitality, retail) are needed to obtain input on level of support, goals, perceived impacts. For economic impact estimation and the effectiveness of leveraging strategies more specific financial data will be needed (e.g., turnover; special promotions; pricing)
Cities; regulators	Direct and continuous engagement with regulators is needed; direct political involvement with events and tourism is highly desirable (e.g. on boards of directors).
	Regulators to provided feedback and data on crime, waste and recycling, water and energy consumption, traffic, use of public transport, fore and safety statistics
Tourism and economic development agencies	Direct engagement with tourism is desirable for tourism-oriented events. Tourism data usually provided through visitor surveys and market-area research. Events need data on visitor motivation, seasonality, travel modes and patterns, activities, spending, preferences, image of events/destination, complaints & satisfaction.
	Possible source of economic forecasting and impact calculators
Environmental agencies and groups	The degree and regularity of input might depend on the nature of events and their perceived impacts. Obtain data on wildlife habitat and populations, landscape effects, waste disposal and recycling efforts; possible source of data on carbon emissions and ecological footprint
Social & cultural agencies and groups; the arts	Might be directly involved as performers
Venues	Essential feedback from venues will include data on use levels, crowding, queuing, security, crime and vandalism, injuries, sales, etc.
Media	Obtain data on effectiveness of advertising, the nature and extent of publicity received (include content analysis)
	Social-media monitoring and netnography to obtain information on likes and dislikes, engagement, word-of-mouth
Educational institutions	Possible collaborators for research, evaluation and volunteer support; obtain feedback on student participation if applicable

The visitor survey is perhaps the most common research and evaluation method, and results can usefully be shared among events if they all use standard questions to obtain comparable data. Development of a shared online visitor survey greatly facilitates standardized data collection and analysis.

Data from all participating events should be stored in a database accessible to approved users (obviously permission is required for this kind of sharing). The database should also hold information from other sources, such as trend analysis and general research that might have value.

Standard questions can be provided in modules, with an optional menu provided to users. When designing the visitor survey, users can pick and chose what is suitable or add their own, but hopefully will include the standard questions.

Study questions

1   In goal-attainment evaluation there can arise tunnel vision. What is the nature of this problem and how is it to be avoided?

2   Explain how the Event Compass implements key elements of the TBL and Balanced Scorecard models. Discuss the measurement problem (or incommensurability) and how the Compass deals with it.

3   Select three key event and tourism stakeholders and explain what goals they might have for a given event, then discuss the data and feedback they can provide for evaluation.

Recommended additional readings and sources

O'Toole, W. (2011). *Events Feasibility and Development: From Strategy to Operations.* Amsterdam: Butterworth-Heinemann.

O'Toole, W. and Mikolaitis, P. (2002). *Corporate Event Project Management.* New York: John Wiley & Son

8 Evaluating the Organisation: (I)

Learning objectives

☐ Know how an event or event-tourism organisation can be evaluated with regard to each of its management functions and its overall effectiveness and success.

☐ Be able to implement ISO principles for effective organisations.

☐ Understand how ownership and mandate are linked.

☐ Know the meaning of governance and its importance for evaluation.

☐ Be able to describe and evaluate an organisation's business model.

☐ Be able to assess the adequacy of administrative services.

☐ Understand the roles of planning and specific types of plan.

8.1 Introduction

In terms of complexity, evaluating the event or event-tourism organisation ranks very high. There will be many stakeholders involved, the issues are sometimes difficult to define, and the scope of evaluation is wide. But this is also why a permanent, comprehensive evaluation system has to be in place.

Consultants are sometimes employed to provide an external evaluation or audit of an organisation, and certifying bodies do it, but ensuring that on-going evaluation and continuous improvement are implemented is the responsibility of directors/owners, with CEOs and other managers having to report regularly on issues and progress.

If the organisation and its management is structurally weak or incompetent, any event they produce or any strategy they pursue is likely to be seriously flawed. However, defining the 'effective organisation' is not in itself easy. It is indeed possible for loosely organised volunteers to produce a great event, with all the mistakes hidden from view (yes, I have been there!). There is not necessarily a one-to-one correlation between sound organisation and successful event outcomes.

In this chapter the starting point is ISO standards, as these provide structure and guidance for an evaluation system that looks at the whole organisation, as opposed to specific issues or problems. So does the Event Compass, described in the previous chapter. Figure 8.1 provides a framework for the remaining sections of this chapter and the next. It clusters inter-related topics into seven categories, but this is for convenience only. Each topic is examined with emphasis on providing pertinent goals, evaluation measures and methods.

Figure 8.1: A framework for evaluating the event organisation

8.2 Standards

The whole purpose of international standards is to ensure that organisations conform to expected standards of policies, procedures, documentation and management systems. For the events sector we have The Global Reporting Initiative Event Organisers Supplement, and international standard ISO 20121: Event Sustainability Management Systems.

According to Meegan Jones, author of the book *Sustainable Event Management, A Practical Guide* (2018), these standards are underscored by the principles of sustainable development such as those prescribed in the UN Global Compact, and embrace social responsibility and principles outlined in ISO 26000 Social Responsibility. They require an organisation to put in place a transparent process through which it systematically evaluates the issues relevant to its operations and sets its own objectives and targets for improvement.

8.2.1 ISO standards for a quality management system

Source: https://www.iso.org/standard/62085.html

All ISO standards have many elements in common. These are generic and can be adapted to any organisation. The sustainability standards have a more specific intent. Notice the emphasis on quality, and keep in mind that it means different things to different organisations. I associate quality with effectiveness.

"ISO 9001:2015 specifies requirements for a quality management system when an organisation:

a) needs to demonstrate its ability to consistently provide products and services that meet customer and applicable statutory and regulatory requirements, and

b) aims to enhance customer satisfaction through the effective application of the system, including processes for improvement of the system and the assurance of conformity to customer and applicable statutory and regulatory requirements."

Commitment to ISO leads to external certification by experts, and implementing an internal auditing system. Internal audits equate with systematic evaluation, not just financial audits. ISO not only leads to systematic quality planning and evaluation but also focuses management's attention on continuous improvement and risk prevention.

8.2.2   ISO principles

Seven principles guide ISO 9001: 2015, and for each of these I have added some pertinent goals and KPIs. Note the similarities with the previously discussed CIPP and Balanced Scorecard Models, and the Event Compass.

Principle 1: Customer focus

All events must take a marketing or customer orientation, even if they are free to invited guests. A marketing or consumer orientation focuses managers' attention on the customer experience, rather than becoming pre-occupied with design, logistics or delivery of a programme. Sometimes guest or customer satisfaction is not the top goal, nor is profit or revenue generation. Owners/managers might very well define quality and success in other ways, such as delivery of community service, client needs, media attention and image making, or tourism-related economic impacts. In the table below both orientations are included. *Clients*, in this context, could include stakeholder groups or constituencies such as people in need, cultural groups, companies, clubs and teams.

Figure 8.2: Suggested customer-focus goals and sample KPIs

Suggested customer-focused goals	Sample KPIs
▪ The guest/customer will always be the focus of our efforts.	▪ Percentage of highly satisfied guests/customers ▪ Complaints reduced over time ▪ Incidents affecting experiences (reduced, ameliorated) ▪ Loyalty (more repeat visits) ▪ More and better word of mouth recommendations
▪ The needs of our community (stakeholders; clients) will always be the focus of our efforts.	▪ Clients and stakeholders satisfied ▪ Growing repeat business ▪ Growing community engagement through volunteering

Principle 2: Leadership

Leaders can be the owners, the board of directors, CEOs and managers – anyone who can influence the organisational culture and make important policy/strategy decisions. Some experts define leadership in terms of the ability to inspire and motivate others, which is a qualitative approach rather than a definition based on power or position. In some cultures strong leaders are not appreciated, and collaborative efforts entailing group decision-making are preferred.

Figure 8.3: Leadership goals and KPIs

Suggested leadership goals	Sample KPIs
A clear mandate and vision will be communicated to all stakeholders, internal and external	▪ Firm knowledge of mandate and mission demonstrated among staff, volunteers and external stakeholders
We will lead in a consultative, transparent style, respectful of all our stakeholder opinions and positions	▪ High stakeholder satisfaction and few complaints

Can leaders evaluate themselves? Usually stakeholder input is needed, covering many perspectives, and external consultants might be necessary to address organisational culture and leadership issues. Event leadership might include volunteers or volunteers working with professionals, so different evaluation methods are required.

Principle 3: Engagement

Stakeholder engagement is likely to be more difficult than it sounds, especially if a wide interpretation of 'legitimate stakeholder' is taken. Just how do you get residents and sponsors, for example, to provide on-going, positive input?

Figure 8.4: Engagement goals and KPIs

Suggested engagement goals	Sample KPIs
All stakeholders will be consulted in planning and evaluation.	▪ High stakeholder satisfaction; few complaints
Staff and volunteers will be empowered to provide an excellent event, solve problems and improve visitor experiences.	▪ High and increasing visitor satisfaction

Principle 4: Process approach

This principle applies to the implementation of a comprehensive and systematic planning and evaluation system, systems thinking about goals, outputs and outcomes. Risk management and contingency planning are included.

Figure 8.5: Process goals and KPIs

Suggested process goals	Sample KPIs
Implement a permanent, comprehensive planning and evaluation system including risk management and contingency plans.	▪ ISO certification will be evidence of compliance ▪ Implementation of the Event Compass or comparable system (this will yield regular reports)
Employ goal-attainment evaluation but always identify unexpected, negative and external costs and impacts.	▪ Production of cost-benefit evaluations constitutes proof of compliance

Principle 5: Improvement

Continuous improvement is accepted as a basic principle of quality management, but it is also the essence of sustainability. It entails identifying, meeting and exceeding or revising goals. It can only work in a learning organisation, open to stakeholder input, and in which innovation is encouraged and supported. A good vision statement will set the stage for improvement.

Figure 8.6: Improvement goals and KPIs

Suggested improvement goals	Sample KPIs
Our vision and strategy will direct innovation and continuous quality improvement	▪ Firm knowledge and acceptance of vision among all stakeholders
Innovation will be fostered through benchmarking, education, knowledge management and stakeholder input.	▪ Innovation can be demonstrated by reference to effective changes in organisation, marketing, design, programming etc. ▪ Formal benchmarking studies will be evidence of intent to innovate

Principle 6 – Evidence-based decision making

The learning organisation utilizes the results of evaluation and makes rational, goal-driven decisions. But do not expect to find this principle being implemented all the time! Irrational decisions abound in all businesses and human affairs. Accountability is part of this principle, with the organisers / owners being accountable internally to staff and volunteers, and externally to the community, regulators, sponsors and other stakeholders.

Figure 8.7: Decision-making goals and KPIs

Suggested decision-making goals	Sample KPIs
Planning and decisions will be made openly, through full consultations, based on evidence, and according to our mandate and vision.	■ High stakeholder satisfaction with the process ■ Evidence-based decision making requires demonstration of market intelligence through research and problem-solving through evaluation
We will be fully accountable to all our stakeholders.	■ All regulatory approvals are obtained ■ High and sustained stakeholder support demonstrated through grants and sponsorships, political support and formal networking or collaborations

Principle 7: Relationship management

This is the essence of both external and internal stakeholder management, as mentioned in some of the above-mentioned principles. It will include procurement and supply-chain management.

Figure 8.8: Relationship management goals and KPIs

Suggested relationship management goals	Sample KPIs
We will fully consult all our internal and external stakeholders and in particular take their evaluations of our events and organisation into account.	Documentation of stakeholder input including external evaluation reports.
We will plan and monitor our supply chain to ensure compliance with our sustainability and ethical standards	Documentation of standards and the contracts (or other evidence of compliance) by suppliers

8.3 Ownership, mandate, governance & business model

These interdependent concepts are a logical starting point for organisational audits, as they set the tone for everything the organisation does. For informal events there will always be key organisers who can provide the necessary information to reveal underlying values, purpose, and structure. Events owned by agencies or large companies might display cross-overs such as the mandate and governance being those of the parent organisation.

In an event-tourism context, some very specific parameters will apply. Most DMOs are created for marketing purposes, but some do produce and own events; mostly they engage in bidding on events and marketing. Event-development corporations tend to have broader mandates and are engaged in a whole range of supportive programmes. See the book *Event Tourism* (Getz, 2013) for a complete discussion and examples.

The type of *ownership* will influence the evaluation of the organisation and be present throughout its management. Why? Because for-profit companies have a simple, unspoken mandate – to make money for owners and investors. Yes, companies should adopt sustainability and social responsibility principles, but if they do not show a reasonable return on investment, they will not remain viable. In the government sector it is necessary to demonstrate public good, and in the not-for-profit or voluntary sector a mix of evaluation criteria can occur, such as generating surplus revenue for charity, social marketing to advance a cause, and fostering community development.

There is another important connotation to the word *ownership*. Mostly it is used in a legal sense, as in "who owns this event"? The owners are responsible, they have obligations, and are accountable to any shareholders. But the term 'community ownership' can be relevant, as in "the event fosters a sense of community ownership". This is usually achieved through widespread support and volunteer engagement. In this context the ownership of the event embodies principles of social responsibility.

Mandate literally means the command or authorization to do something, as in "your mandate as event organisers is to implement the Council's policies on tourism and social integration." Mandates are inherent in ownership, but an explicit statement is best in order to avoid confusion.

The term *mission* can be used, and those in the not-for-profit sector might prefer the connotation that they are on a mission to do good. 'Mission' can imply values, and that is the main difference from 'mandate'.

Business model is not to be confused with the business plan. Ownership suggests the mandate, but the business model goes beyond. A business model is a design or plan for successful operation, its key elements being financial viability (what are the revenue sources?), a customer base (guests or paying customers?), products/services (the programme or experience proposition), and a management system (volunteer-based or professional, permanent or one-time only?).

A business model explains how the organisation creates and captures value, whether defined by profit or service. It entails appropriate ownership and decision making, a mandate or mission statement, marketing orientation, and the nature of its service propositions.

Figure 8.9: Ownership, mandate, business model and governance goals and KPIs

Suggested goals for ownership, mandate & business model	Sample KPIs
■ Create a clear statement of mandate or mission, expressing values and purpose of the event	■ High degree of public support
■ Create value for the community through public service AND/OR create value through attracting tourists and leveraging events for business growth	■ Positive media coverage
	■ Documentation of various forms of public and stakeholder consultations
■ Engage the community to foster a sense of ownership and commitment	■ Official press releases and accountability reports of the organisation
■ Be accountable to owners and other key stakeholders	■ Impact assessments as evidence of effectiveness in creating value
	■ Satisfaction of all stakeholders

Suggested goals for governance	Sample KPIs
■ Ensure a competent, representative board of directors	■ Interviews with stakeholders and directors to confirm inclusion
■ Bring key stakeholders into the ownership and/or leadership team	■ Certification will indicate organisational competence
	■ Objective leadership reviews are conducted; recommendations have been implemented

8.3.1 Governance

"Governance determines who has power, who makes decisions, how other players make their voice heard and how account is rendered."

Source: The Institute on Governance: http://iog.ca/defining-governance/

In the above definition "how account is rendered" is equivalent to 'accountability'.

Owners govern private companies, although they may decide to involve stakeholders – including staff. Some people believe that private businesses and event organisations need a 'social license to operate', consisting of goodwill and acknowledgement of legitimacy, but this is a contentious issue. In most countries private companies have laws unto themselves and do not need widespread public support to exist, although it is probably needed to remain successful.

Not-for-profit organisations are typically governed by boards of directors, although there is considerable variation in how directors are selected. Societies and clubs usually hold elections from formal membership, while some events will simply ask people to serve. Active engagement with multiple stakeholders, including residents and interest groups is more a hallmark of the non-profit sector. In the public sector the dominant form of event governance will be local, elected officials, although they can appoint directors and managers to do the real work.

Whitford, Phi and Dredge (2014), in a paper that won the Donald Getz Award for best paper in the journal *Event Management*, developed indicators for measuring governance performance in events.

Research Note

Whitford, M., Phi, G. & Dredge, D. (2014). Principles to practice: Indicators for measuring event governance performance. *Event Management* **18**, 387–403.

Abstract: Governments are increasingly involved in public–private partnerships to attract, support, and/or stage events. This involvement often leads to governments becoming embroiled in highly politicized battles that focus on issues including community benefit, mitigation of impacts, transparency in decision making, and lack of consultation before, during, and after the event. To date, minimal attention has been paid to the public–private governance arrangements underpinning events. This article seeks to address this gap by presenting a set of indicators that can be operationalized to improve event governance.

Whitford, Phi and Dredge provided a series of indicators that can be used by event evaluators, reflecting the following major governance principles (with my comments added):

♦ *Transparency:* governance should be open to public scrutiny; decisions are justified; adherence to law, regulations and codes of ethical conduct is essential

♦ *Responsiveness and equitable participation*: stakeholders are consulted; the public has real influence on decisions; groups are not marginalised

♦ *Structure:* consideration of how institutions and stakeholders are networked, giving rise to either imbalances of power or access to decision makers

♦ *Accountability:* is it open and honest? do events and DMOs publish full cost-benefit evaluations? can people demand information about finances and operations?

8.4 Adminstration

This term is used in different ways, sometimes simply to describe the various office functions associated with keeping an organisation functioning, like secretarial services, paper work, documentation, filing, answering phones, etc. It can also refer to the people who govern, as in "the administrators" of the event determine its strategy. And it can mean the implementation of mandate or policy, as in "the board governs and the staff administer" or "the finance officer has the responsibility to administer all our contracts".

Probably the best definition, in the context of evaluation, is "having necessary systems in place to ensure fulfilment of the organisation's mission" as that includes evaluation. Meeting the ISO standards will suffice to cover the meanings of administration.

Figure 8.10: Administration goals and KPIs

Suggested goals for administration	Sample KPIs
▪ Provide the systems and office support necessary for systematic evaluation and continuous improvement. ▪ Maintain documents to demonstrate compliance with applicable standards	▪ ISO certification or adoption of a system like Event Compass will provide the measures of effectiveness in attaining these goals

8.5 Planning

Planning without an integrated evaluation system makes no sense, at least not for learning organisations and those seeking continuous improvement. Ironically, the evaluators also have to audit the planning system and their own contributions to it. If that poses a risky conflict of interest, then outside consultants will be needed.

To set goals and KPIs as recommended in this book is, in effect, planning. In other words if you start evaluating goal attainment you are automatically contributing to strategy and other forms of planning. Evaluation of planning has to take into account the range of planning activities and formal plans that an organisation might undertake, as each presents different challenges. Initial questions include:

♦ Do we have these plans as documents, or are the planning processes informal?

♦ What is missing from our planning system?

♦ Who is involved in planning and evaluation?

♦ Are all desired inputs obtained from internal and external stakeholders?

♦ Are plans comprehensive and clear?

♦ Are plans communicated effectively to the right people?

♦ How will we measure effectiveness? That is, have we the evaluation system in place to determine successes, failures, threats, etc.?

♦ Are plans regularly reviewed and updated? By whom? How?

Project planning applies to one-time events and to informal or weakly organised events that start all over again each time they are produced. The key evaluation tasks are monitoring and control to ensure the event is produced on time and on schedule. The project management team might also be responsible for the wrap-up (i.e., shutting down the organisation) and final accounts, but there could be a separation of planners, event producers, and those doing final accounts.

Strategic planning is necessary in permanent organisations and for recurring events that hope to prosper. The strategy starts with mandate, usually includes a vision statement (i.e., where we want to be in a period of time), goals, performance measures (i.e., KPIs or objectives) and an action plan with responsibilities and resources specified. Some managers prefer regular updates and flexibility (they might believe in "emergent strategies" that evolve in line with continuous feedback and improvement) while others stick to a blueprint. Management theorists and gurus differ in their approach to strategy, but every organisation has one, whether it is implicit in its actions or explicitly expressed in a document.

Business planning combines strategies, actions and budgets in a document that can be used to persuade lenders, grant-givers, sponsors and other stakeholders that the organisers know exactly what they are doing, and they can be trusted to get the event or project delivered as planned. There are numerous sources available for constructing and using the business plan.

Sensitivity analysis can be used as an evaluation tool in a number of circumstances. The basic questions to ask: what will any deviation in forecast revenue or expenditure do to our bottom line? Will a deviation of a certain percentage mean that we do not break even or make the target profit level?

Marketing and communications planning takes its lead from strategy and will often consist of an action plan with budget for gathering market intelligence (including original research), target marketing (by identifying segments and their needs) advertising and other communications. An expanded view would include all relations with external stakeholders and "internal marketing" with staff and volunteers, but I consider these to be part of stakeholder management. A section on marketing follows.

Setting and site planning: The setting could be a park and the specific site a stage plus viewing area. Meetings mostly require indoor spaces with a variety of seating arrangements. Sports have specified venues such as playing fields that cannot be altered, but the surroundings are designed.

Operations planning is all about getting the event produced, including *logistics* (the timely movement of people, vehicles, goods, money, information and equipment), procurement, scheduling, site planning, and everything needed for an event to offer a great experience. Failures will become quite evident during events, as when equipment does not arrive, toilets run out of soap, long queues form at the gate, injuries happen, people get sick, and on and on. Evaluation methods include observation and de-briefings, incident reports, customer and stakeholder feedback. The service blueprint sets specifications, while service mapping provides the feedback.

Management of Event Operations (Tum, Norton and Wright, 2006) provides details on event planning, supply-chain and risk management, forecasting, capacity, implementation, and performance evaluation. They recommend a 'control cycle' consisting of four steps: setting standard specifications, feedback on actual performance, measurement of performance against the specification, and correction of deviations.

Figure 8.11: Planning goals and KPIs

Suggested goals for planning	Sample KPIs
Strategic planning ■ Formulate and constantly revise a strategic plan ■ Pay attention to emergent strategies reflecting what works and does not work ■ Develop clear statements of mission (or mandate), and a long-term vision ■ Develop goals and objectives (or performance measures) ■ Demonstrate continuous learning through evaluation and research, including benchmarking ■ Meet the requirements of ISO 20121 (Event Sustainability Management Systems).	A formal strategic plan should cover all these goals, otherwise the evaluator has to take a goal-free, systems approach to determining what the organisation is doing and how effective it has been. KPIs: ■ Acceptance of, and support for the strategy by all key stakeholders ■ Certification obtained and renewed ■ Success criteria such as: best in class (compared to other events); longevity; growth; reputation; brand recognition

Project Planning	▪ Zero deviations from critical path (i.e., all tasks completed on time)
▪ Utilize available project planning software	▪ Implementation of the plan and schedule as measured by staff/volunteer adherence to schedule and tasks
▪ Utilize project planning and management tools for programming, setting (i.e., Site planning), service provision/quality, and consumables (food/beverages, merchandise, gifts)	Utilizing project management software with critical path scheduling will certainly assist in meeting these goals.
▪ Develop and adhere to a critical path for production of the event	
Operations planning (including logistics)	▪ Logistical efficiency: measured through analysis of service failures, people and vehicle movement, unexpected delays and costs
▪ Implement systems and set standard specifications for supply-chain management, customer service/quality, information and communications, technical support, security, and financial controls	▪ Stakeholder buy-in: especially adherence to goals by suppliers
▪ Manage all flows of money, material, people and information/communications in order to reduce risks	▪ Efficiency: set targets for wait/queuing times
▪ Improve traffic flow and parking	▪ Meet quality targets: pertinent evidence from risk evaluation and customer feedback, plus observations
▪ Increase reliance on public transport	▪ Evidence of problems from external reports (e.g., police)
▪ Secure and utilize feedback from all stakeholders to improve operations -develop a logistics plan for the management of flows and traffic (see operations)	▪ Evidence from incident reports

Some very useful evaluation tools are illustrated in *Management of Event Operations* (Tum et al., 2006), part of what is generically referred to as 'root-cause' analysis. The 'Ishikawa Diagram' starts with recognition of a problem and works backwards to identify causes. For example, was the inadequacy of lighting due to personnel (e.g., lack of empowerment or inadequate training?), resources (time constraints, no money, inadequate venue?), communications (with venue manager or staff?) or perhaps an electrical failure? The 'fishbone diagram' starts with a problem and, in contrast, seeks to identify consequences. For example, at a free event if more people than expected show up (this scenario is part of contingency planning) what happens? The consequences might be vehicular congestion, long line-ups, disgruntled customers/guests, and unhappy residents of the area.

The two types of diagram can be combined, as illustrated in Figure 8.12. On the 'Causes?' I have used the eight Ps of the marketing mix (based on Morrison, 1995, and discussed in Getz, 2005) with the experiential Ps on top and the facilitating Ps on the bottom. This will work as a starting point for most event-specific problems, but note that each element can be subdivided – such as training under People and lack of sponsors under Partnerships. On the 'Consequences?' side I have suggested looking for both external and internal impacts. If the example is "too many guests showed up", the causes might lie both in marketing and inadequate venues, while the consequences might include additional car traffic and therefore more carbon emissions. In other words, the evaluators have to keep digging deeper and extend their analysis of both causes and effects beyond internal factors.

Figure 8.12: Root-cause and impact forecasting combined

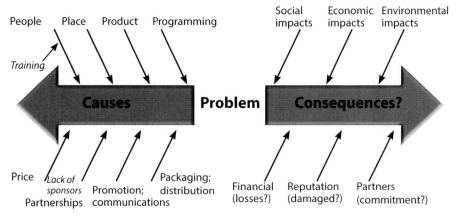

Figure 8.13: The Evaluator's Toolbox: Ishikawa and Fishbone diagrams; decision trees

Evaluation tools	Applications
Root-Cause Analysis: Systematic identification of the causes of problems or potential deviations from standards.	Start with a problem and work backwards to seek causes, many of which will involve multiple, interdependent factors. Apply to all service failures and deviations from standards.
Ishikawa Diagram: The problem is identified and the team/evaluators works backwards looking for causes.	The evaluator should have some pre-knowledge of what might lead to the problem.
Fishbone Diagram: The problem is identified and the team/evaluators examine possible consequences and solutions (or amelioration)	This is partly impact forecasting and partly contingency planning. It can also form part of the goal-attainment 'logic model'.

Study questions

1 How would you evaluate the potential effectiveness and success of an event or a tourism organisation, based on its ownership, governance and compliance with standards? What do you think are the critical success factors?

2 Describe specific evaluation challenges and appropriate methods for each type of planning applicable to events and event tourism.

3 Design a problem-solving process (with diagram) for a likely problem faced in events or event tourism. How will evaluation inform the ultimate decision?

Recommended additional readings and sources

The Institute on Governance: http://iog.ca/defining-governance/

Tum, J., Norton, P., & Wright, J. (2006). *Management of Event Operations*. Amsterdam: Butterworth-Heinemann.

9 Evaluating the Organisation (II)

Learning objectives

☐ Be able to evaluate an organisation regarding its meeting of standards and as to its effectiveness by examining its main management functions, as follows:

- Design
- Management and decision-support information systems; knowledge management
- Financial management and control; business planning
- Risk assessment and management
- Human resources; human-resource planning
- Marketing and communications; marketing planning
- Sustainability and social responsibility.

☐ Be aware of how organisations, events, and programmes can naturally follow (or be designed to follow) a life cycle from creation to termination and how this affects planning and evaluation.

9.1 Design

Design as a process, like planning, starts with goals; or, what is the problem, and how do we come up with the best solution? Design includes both technical and artistic/creative elements, working in harmony. Theatrical sets and stages are designed to both aesthetic and technical specifications. Event sites are designed to meet both logistical and experiential goals.

As emphasized by Berridge, author of *Events Design and Experience* (2007), it is necessary to ask to what extent an event experience can be designed? He argued that it cannot be left to chance and that design must be fully integrated in the concept, structure and execution of an event.

Design has to be hierarchical: a part of concept development, setting and site planning, venues and décor. It will influence marketing and communications, including the brand and image-making. In large part the effectiveness of design will be a subjective evaluation, as in: "can we do better?" Much of the evaluation evidence will come from customer satisfaction measures and the stakeholders who can provide technical feedback.

Figure 9.1: Design goals and KPIs

Suggested design goals	Sample KPIs
Programme design ■ Create a unique theme and programme ■ Develop a programme plan and schedule ■ Co-create experiences with customers ■ Foster programming innovation	■ High level of customer satisfaction ■ Internal design excellence as judged by staff, volunteers, managers and stakeholders ■ Comparative design excellence: independent quality evaluations by experts, including benchmarking ■ Acceptance of programming changes by customers and other key stakeholders
Setting design (Including site planning, aesthetics and decor; links directly to operations and logistics) ■ Prepare and implement a site plan ■ Develop a decoration theme and detailed design	■ Customer/guest satisfaction ■ Achievement of surprise and creation of the omg! Or wow! factor (observation and direct feedback from guests) ■ Excellence of design judged by comparisons or experts (an aesthetics audit?)
Service design (Covering all systems for staff and volunteer interactions with guests, customers or participants; also covers VIP and performer services) ■ Employ service blueprinting or other methods to plan and deliver the highest possible level of customer satisfaction ■ Evaluate customer experiences and satisfaction to achieve continuous improvement	■ Zero service failures as defined by blueprint specifications; or set targets for reduction ■ Continuous improvement in customer satisfaction levels; set targets ■ Reduce complaints; set targets Must be tied to HR evaluation (i.e., performance standards for staff and volunteers)
Consumables design (Covers food and beverages, gifts and souvenirs, merchandise) ■ Demonstrate adherence to all applicable standards and regulations (e.g., food safety) ■ Achieve high levels of customer satisfaction ■ Evaluate customer/guest experiences and their direct feedback to ensure continuous improvement ■ Work with suppliers to make mutually beneficial improvements	■ Zero service failures (i.e., no health or safety problems) ■ Licensing compliance (usually requires independent inspections) ■ High customer/guest satisfaction ■ Demonstrated improvements (requires benchmark data and a plan)

In Figure 9.1 design is sub-divided into these categories: programme, setting, service, and consumables. The *programme* consists of the theme and the activities or experiences of those participating in the event. This means the actual sport (spectator or participant) or arts and entertainment (again, for participants or spectators). For business events it includes the educational and social sessions, and the activities associated with exhibiting and marketing. Programmes are scheduled, but there are always informal activities and unplanned experiences occurring at events that should also be evaluated.

Quality standards should be set for all these elements, with the guest, participants and customers usually the main source of evidence for quality evaluations.

Programme quality is usually the dominant consideration when it comes to customer satisfaction, whereas service quality (mainly the interactions between attendees and the setting and staff/volunteers) can generate specific complaints. Chapters 10 and 11 cover evaluation of experiences and quality in greater detail.

9.2 Management and decision-support information systems; knowledge management

Information management is really a technical process employing records and computer systems, while knowledge management starts with the culture and implementation of principles of the 'learning organisation'. It encompasses formal learning and professional development, innovation, and tacit knowledge (i.e., facts, and what is understood by personnel and stakeholders – namely wisdom). What is needed to support decisions is a combination of the two.

Evaluation is an integral part of this process, but the results of research and evaluation have to be applied, and that requires the experience and wisdom of people. The standardization and sharing of research, market intelligence and evaluation/ impact assessments will greatly enhance learning and improve decision making, which makes a strong case for collaborations and portfolio management.

Figure 9.2: Information and knowledge management goals and KPIs

Suggested goals: information systems and knowledge management	Sample KPIs
■ Provide necessary information for all management functions through research, monitoring, environmental scanning, benchmarking & evaluation. ■ Facilitate the documentation and sharing of experiences and knowledge among personnel, and its perpetuation as 'institutional memory'.	■ Elimination of data and knowledge gaps (which can only be demonstrated on an as-needed basis) ■ The documentation and accessibility of all data, research and evaluation findings ■ Training effectiveness (i.e., with regard to passing on experiences and wisdom)

9.3 Financial management and business planning

Financial accounts are a given, as most organisations are required to have them done professionally every year. The organisation's accountants will certify the statements, while internally five different financial 'accounts' are maintained:

- ◆ Asset
- ◆ Liability
- ◆ Equity
- ◆ Revenue
- ◆ Expense

The financial data and statements do not in themselves constitute evaluation, rather they provide input to answering vital questions such as:

♦ Are we financially solvent or healthy?

♦ Do we have resources to re-invest?

♦ Are we a profitable business?

♦ What is our value if we sell?

Figure 9.3: Financial management and business planning goals and KPIs

Suggested goals for financial management and business planning	Sample KPIs
Business planning ■ Secure committed, long-term funding ■ Generate a surplus ■ Develop and maintain a reserve fund ■ Develop and implement realistic capital and operating budgets ■ Develop and implement effective financial controls ■ Conduct ratio analysis ■ Value all assets, including the event as a sponsorship platform ■ Measure adherence to the budget ■ Measure profit and losses ■ Manage all assets and the supply chain to continuously improve efficiency (e.g., in terms of labour, supplies, energy, water, money) ■ Improve technological and information inputs to increase efficiency and effectiveness ■ Maximise use of volunteers	A formal Business Plan including a realistic budget is evidence of business planning. Formal financial audits provide solid evidence of effectiveness and efficiency. Each of the goals suggests at least one KPI: ■ Set a target for an operating surplus or ROI ■ Maintain a reserve fund ■ Zero financial losses owing to theft, loss, waste ■ Accumulating assets (e.g., land, equipment, venues) ■ Efficiency gains measured through various ratios ■ Determine a financial value for volunteer labour based on equivalent staff pay rates

9.3.1 Efficiency

Business managers are always concerned about increasing efficiency, but it should be a concern to everyone in the organisation. These three questions reflect major efficiency issues:

♦ Can we increase output (or better meet our goals) with less input (mainly money, but also labour or marketing effort).

♦ Is it possible to get more (e.g. paying customers) for the same effort or investment?

♦ If we spent more time/money/effort could we make significantly more money (or do a much better job attaining goals)?

Operational efficiency (an overall metric for the event or organisation) can be defined as the ratio of outputs to inputs. Many businesses use money, obviously, but for government and not-for-profit organisations output will have a different meaning, related to purpose and goal attainment – the logic is the same. Some possible output metrics: revenue, profit margin, cash, new customers, customer loyalty, market differentiation, production, innovation, quality, sustainability, stakeholder support.

Productivity is a related concept and can be defined as a measure of how much output is generated by a unit of input. For workers at an event, that could be difficult to determine. In certain circumstances objective measures of productivity are feasible, such as how many staff/volunteer hours it takes to sell tickets at the gate and get everyone into a venue. The question then becomes, how can this productivity level be improved?

9.4 Risk management

'Hazards' are everywhere – the bad things that might happen – and 'risks' are the probability that they will happen. The usual terminology, however, is to talk about 'risk management'. Silvers, in the book *Risk Management for Meetings and Events* (2008) listed typical risk factors for events, from activities to timing and scheduling, and provided details on risk management including the functions of monitoring, evaluation and documentation. Knowing the full range of hazards is a logical starting point for the evaluator. In addition, each event and event type entails risks peculiar to their combination of setting, management systems, people and programme that have to be learned.

O'Toole (2011) called for a 'risk register', and this idea suggests the importance of integrating risk identification and management with all management, planning and design functions. Pulled into one document available to all stakeholders, the risk register will become a guide to evaluation and response, and with regular updates based on experience it becomes part of the learning organisation's fundamental teaching resources. Obviously one component in the register will be the risk assessment and contingency plans. Another will be critical incident reports. Performance standards or KPIs should also be part of the register – for example, how long should it take to evacuate an audience or treat an injury?

The legal principle of 'due diligence' requires full documentation of the risk management plan and actions taken to minimize or avoid risks. Staff and volunteers therefore have to be trained to achieve competence in all aspects of risk management.

Figure 9.4 lists the main stages in risk planning and management, with appropriate goals and suggested KPIs.

Figure 9.4: Risk management goals and KPIs   Key Performance indicators

Suggested goals for risk management	Sample KPIs
Identify and categorize risks ■ Conduct regular audits of risks to and from visitor and worker health and safety, the community, event finances, suppliers, sponsors, the environment, infrastructure, organisation and event marketing and brand/reputation ■ Establish on-going consultation with insurers and other experts regarding risks (including benchmarking)	■ Documentation of risk assessments ■ Elimination of identified risks or implementation of strategies to reduce or share risks ■ Reduced insurance claims
Assign probabilities ■ Undertake regular forecasts of risk probabilities	■ Reduction (or elimination) of the probability of identified risks
Assess potential consequences ■ Undertake regular assessments of the severity of risk consequences ■ Emergency response evaluations (incident reporting) ■ Onsite discovery and correction systems for problems ■ Prepare and update emergency plans for response to all identified risks	■ Reduction of negative consequences of identified risks ■ Prompt and complete incident reports ■ Effectiveness of personal and contingency plans, as measured by (for example) reduced monetary losses, less-severe injuries, elimination of safety hazards
Determine priorities ■ Rank risks for prioritised action considering both probability and severity of consequences	■ Continuous re-assessment of priorities based on evaluation ■ Lessening of the priority status of hazards as they become effectively dealt with

Strategies
 ■ Implement policies and procedures to:
  ■ Avoid undesirable and unmanageable risks
  ■ Reduce risk probability and potential consequences
 ■ Share or re-assign risks, as feasible
 ■ Insure against losses and damages
 ■ Prepare for damages or losses (contingency planning)
	The effectiveness of risk management strategies can be evaluated by reference to:
	 ■ Reduction or elimination of specific losses, accidents, damages (i.e., set targets)

Compliance ■ Prepare and implement a compliance protocol (regulations, security requirements, insurance, contracts)	■ Compliance certificates: compliance with regulations is a legal matter; review regularly with key stakeholders

Pertinent checklists are provided in the Silvers book and in public documents such as the Fire Safety Risk Assessment by the UK Department for Communities and Local Government Publications (2007), pertaining to emergency exits. The evaluator, in this case perhaps an 'emergency measures officer', is responsible for numerous procedures related to security and safety at events.

9.5 Human resources

Chapter 12 is devoted to human resource evaluation. The full HR planning and management process must be subjected to permanent evaluation, including planning, organisational design for effective HR management, recruitment, training, performance evaluation, discipline, termination, re-enlistment.

Figure 9.5: Human resource management goals and KPIs

Suggested goals for human resource management	Sample KPIs
Planning ■ Establish comprehensive HR policies and procedures, integrate with overall planning and project management ■ Develop an effective recruitment, induction, training and motivation plan (e.g., for rewards and retention) ■ Establish performance evaluation methods and measures through consultation with staff and volunteers ■ Constantly review and update job descriptions ■ Structure the organisation so that staff and volunteers are placed appropriately, considering their needs and abilities	■ HR plans, policies and procedures meet ISO standards ■ The primary KPI for effective HR planning is a satisfied, committed workforce (staff and volunteers)
Recruitment, motivation and training ■ Constantly evaluate and improve the effectiveness of recruitment and training (with real-time adjustments as necessary) ■ Obtain feedback to ensure that staff and volunteer needs and motives are understood and acted upon	■ Reduce turnover (monitor staff and volunteer turnover rates) ■ Fill all positions ■ Satisfy staff/volunteer needs
Work environment ■ Ensure constant compliance with all workplace health and safety standards and regulations ■ Assign clear responsibilities for risk assessment, critical incident response and evaluation/correction procedures ■ Employ performance reviews to help improve the working environment ■ Ensure a satisfied, committed workforce	■ Conduct annual self-evaluations and supervisor reports on all staff and volunteers; measure satisfaction, complaints, goals, suggestions ■ Establish and annually assess incident reports; include accidents, ethical issues and complaints in the system; provide support (e.g., counselling)
Professionalism and ethics ■ Develop and enforce ethical standards to cover all aspects of the event, its organisation and workforce ■ Through hiring and training, continuously improve the credentials and skills of staff and volunteers	■ Continuous feedback from staff, volunteers, supervisors and stakeholders on ethical issues to eliminate incidents or complaints ■ Testing of training effectiveness on knowledge and compliance

9.6 Marketing and communications

Marketing effectiveness is one focus of evaluators, but how is the entire marketing and communications function to be evaluated at the organisational level? There has to be a learning culture in which market intelligence is valued, a marketing or consumer orientation (as opposed to merely trying to sell a product/event), and a plan for marketing and communications. The entire marketing mix must be open to evaluation.

Figure 9.6: Marketing and communication goals and KPIs

Suggested goals for marketing and communications	Sample KPIs
Marketing (or consumer) orientation ▪ Engage with guests/customers to co-create satisfying memorable experiences ▪ Cater to both generic leisure/tourist motivation and provide event-specific reasons to travel/attend ▪ Be iconic (i.e., symbolic values stressed) for targeted, special-interest groups ▪ Become a valued tradition for residents (i.e., hallmark event) ● Obtain and utilize timely market intelligence on demand, needs, preferences ▪ Determine visitor needs and motives ▪ Maintain a fresh, competitive event (or portfolio)	▪ Satisfied and loyal visitors ▪ Desired behaviours realised (sales, etc.) ▪ Positive sponsors' evaluation ▪ Positive resident perceptions & attitudes ▪ Strong competitive position Sources of data: ▪ Visitor/attendee surveys ▪ Media audit ▪ On-site sales records ▪ Tax records ▪ Sponsors' feedback ▪ Resident survey, focus groups or political feedback

Marketing and communications strategy and plan
▪ Conduct research to identify and profile appropriate target segments, including (when appropriate) tourists
▪ Support the refinement of segmentation and target marketing based on visitor and market-area surveys
▪ Devise strategies and communications for each target segment (including mass, targeted, and social media)
▪ Formulate and implement an integrated branding strategy that communicates our values
● Develop and continuously refine a sponsorship strategy to maximise stakeholder engagement and tangible support
	▪ Visitor profiles should match target segments
	▪ Communications effectiveness measures to include:
	    ▪ Demonstrate the reach of communications to target segments
	    ▪ Recognition of brand and brand values
	    ▪ Sponsor loyalty and tangible contributions
	▪ Feedback required from each sponsor as to their ROI
	▪ Event's sales volumes and ROI on merchandising

Marketing mix
▪ Augment marketing efforts through partnerships (e.g., with sponsor, destination, other events)
▪ Utilize appropriate distribution channels to sell and convey merchandise and tickets
▪ Develop and continuously refine our marketing mix strategy, pertaining to:
    Product
    Place
    Programming
    People
    Packaging
    Partnerships
    Public relations (communications)
    Price
	Quantify media coverage and evaluate effectiveness by reference to:
	▪ Conversion rates
	▪ Awareness levels; intention to visit
	▪ Market share (relative to other events)
	▪ Images held by target segments
	▪ Demand trends (relative to price)
	▪ Satisfaction of visitors and stakeholders
	▪ Comparative profitability of different distribution modes (e.g., packaging, direct sales, sponsorship co-marketing)
	▪ Image compared to competitors
	Quantify the relative importance of mass and social media, internet word-of-mouth)

9.7 'Greening' and sustainability

A starting point for evaluation of sustainability has been published (Getz, 2017) and is slightly adapted here for evaluators. It begins with "going green" and then advances into a number of policy fields that reflect the desire for events and tourism to make a positive contribution to sustainable communities. These have to be combined with financial management and social responsibility to comprise a TBL approach to sustainability.

Figure 9.7: Sustainability and greening goals and KPIs

Reccomended sustainability goals	Sample KPIs
AIR: ■ Reduce carbon emissions by maximizing use of public mass transit and by careful targeting of tourist segments ■ Improve air quality	■ Reduced carbon footprint (requires a carbon calculator and data on travel) ■ Percentage of visitors not using private cars (i.e., should be decreased) ■ Air quality standards met (e.g., emissions of all equipment)
WATER: ■ Conserve supplies; reduce use ■ Ensure clean water for all citizens & visitors ■ Prevent water pollution ■ Plant trees & use native organic materials	■ Reduced consumption (set targets) ■ Education of guests leading to changed behaviour ■ Zero water and ground-water pollution ■ Provide drinking water as a service
WASTE: ■ Minimize waste requiring off-site disposal (e.g., food, paper, plastic) ■ Regulate suppliers to avoid unnecessary packaging and non-recyclable material ■ Maximise re-usability of supplies ■ Maximise organics composted	■ Reduced waste (set targets) ■ Maximise re-use; composting
ENERGY: ■ Reduce consumption; ■ Develop alternative, clean sources	■ Reduce consumption; use clean sources; evaluate machinery & equipment for efficiency gains; work with venues to be carbon neutral ■ Reduced ecological footprint (takes all consumption into account, not just energy)
TRANSPORTATION: Maximize use of public, mass transit; reduce auto use and congestion; use clean fuels	■ Reduce private car travel; use shuttle and public mass transit services
NATURE / ECOLOGICAL SYSTEMS: ■ Reduce overall ecological footprint ■ Conserve nature and increase access to nature reserves	■ Educate guests regarding nature conservation; donate money to conservation projects; plant trees; avoid erosion and land pollution; utilize ecological footprint calculator
BUILT ENVIRONMENT & LIVABILITY: Conserve heritage through the design and use of public spaces; achieve safer, quieter, more livable communities	■ Contribute to the livability of communities through design and heritage conservation initiatives; monitor and reduce light and noise pollution; ensure safety and convenience of residents

ECONOMIC DEVELOPMENT: Foster innovation and entrepreneurship; create and preserve jobs; attract investment; foster a progressive business environment; grow responsible tourism	▪ Develop an economic impact strategy and evaluation mechanisms; grow the event and/or expand diversity; become an innovation and creative-city leader; add value through supply-chain management, favouring local and regional suppliers
TOURISM: Target high-yield visitors; overcome seasonality of demand; build and maintain a strong reputation and brand; develop a portfolio of events and venues for long-term, sustainable benefits	▪ Carefully target high-yield tourists; favour off-peak timing; co-brand with the city/destination; stress long-term, sustainable value-creation within a managed event portfolio; evaluate visitor satisfaction
FOOD: Ensure food supplies; develop urban gardening; preserve traditions and maximize culinary authenticity	▪ Implement a food policy favouring authenticity and local/regional suppliers; integrate with RRR actions
EDUCATION /TRAINING: Educate residents and students on sustainability issues and initiatives they can take	▪ Educate guests regarding sustainability issues and practices; train event evaluators
SOCIAL POLICY: Maximize social integration and harmony; foster community development; provide adequate housing for all; build institutions	▪ Set social goals and evaluate outcomes on residents, social groups and the community; engage many stakeholders in social planning
COMMUNITY DEVELOPMENT: Assist communities in dealing with problems, taking sustainability initiatives, and planning their future; ensure leisure opportunities and accessibility for all residents	▪ Develop and manage community stakeholder relations to maximize benefits; increase community self sufficiency through event production
ARTS AND CULTURAL POLICY: Foster arts appreciation and participation; preserve valued traditions; promote tolerance and appreciation of differences	▪ Utilize local talent; preserve cultural traditions; set and evaluate cultural goals
HEALTH: Maximize accessibility to quality health services; prevent disease & injury; encourage responsible, healthy lifestyles	▪ Provide safe, healthy and secure events; encourage positive lifestyle changes
SAFETY and SECURITY: Ensure public safety through traffic controls and crime prevention	▪ Work with police and other security-related agencies to ensure a safe event experience for all

9.8 Social responsibility (CSR)

Social responsibility goals and actions will vary greatly with the type of event and its ownership, with public agencies and not-for-profits generally taking a service orientation that requires accountability to client groups and the public. CSR can start with philanthropy, carefully selecting charitable projects to support, or working with stakeholders and community groups to ensure that events and tourism are relevant to local needs and sensitive to residents' concerns. More fully, CSR can be a guiding strategy for events and tourism agencies, ensuring that the event sector is a positive force for sustainable communities.

Figure 9.8: Social responsibility goals and KPIs

Suggested goals for social responsibility	Sample KPIs
■ Raise money for local charities and community projects.	■ Actual monetary contributions
■ Provide volunteers, and support other volunteer initiatives in our community.	■ Numbers of volunteers provided
■ Adhere to socially-responsible business practices, such as fair trade, and ensure that our suppliers do the same.	■ Fair trade certification ■ Applying sustainability and CSR standards to suppliers
■ Fund or initiate advocacy campaigns (i.e., social marketing for important causes).	■ Stakeholder evaluations of effectiveness

9.9 Life-cycles and evaluation

Periodic events and event organisations both can experience a life cycle from birth to death – and possible reinvention. There is no certainty about this, however, and failures and deliberate terminations in the events world are common. Some periodic events simply run out of energy, particularly owing to volunteer burnout.

Within the theoretical frame of organisational ecology, competition for resources is a primary reason for failures. When resources are plentiful, including start-up funds and customer demand, many events can prosper. When economic times are tough, weak ones can disappear – indeed, financial inadequacies are probably the number one cause of unplanned failures. To ensure longevity events have to find a niche and protect it. Some will pursue a strategy of institutionalisation, becoming *hallmark events* and securing permanent commitment from the key stakeholders – albeit at the expense of some autonomy.

In terms of product life cycles, basically a marketing concept, the introduction, growth and eventual replacement of a specific product or brand is common but not inevitable. 'New Improved' are buzzwords to show potential customers that continuous improvement is a goal.

In a managed portfolio of events, each event is an asset that has to contribute to overall RPI and fill one or more particular roles (such as attracting target segments or providing off-peak attractiveness to the destination). Portfolio managers (such as destination marketing companies or city culture/leisure agencies) viewing events as assets might very well decide that some can be sacrificed, even while new ones are brought on stream. The deliberate termination of funding, or outright cancellation of events that are owned by agencies, might lead to outrage or a public backlash, so it has to be done cautiously.

When evaluating an event organisation, or in strategic planning, there are indicators to look for that, taken together, can reveal much about the life cycle. This is not done specifically for predictive reasons (e.g., "we will fail in three years!") but more as a reflection on what strategies and actions are needed to stay healthy and competitive, financially viable and relevant.

In the hypothetical product life cycle model distinct stages are identified. Sales, revenue or profit are measures frequently used as indicators, with trends to be graphed. There might be a lag between increasing sales and increasing profits. Before the product is even available for sales, research, development and investment are required. This does fit with many planned events, although sales/profits can be substituted with attendance, sponsorship and grant revenue, or perhaps customer and stakeholder satisfaction.

Figure 9.9: Life-cycle goals and KPIs

Suggested goals pertaining to the life cycle of events	Sample KPIs
■ Assess and forecast financial and technical feasibility before introducing new events or programmes ■ Employ scenario making and financial sensitivity analysis to foresee potential risks ■ Obtain constant feedback from guests/ customers and other stakeholders to warn of problems and risks ■ Re-visit strategy periodically in light of changing conditions	■ Discrepancies between forecasts and actual performance ■ Monitoring demand (attendance trends, response to price changes) ■ Trends in customer satisfaction and loyalty ■ Extent of competition (other events, attractions and their growth) ■ Advice from stakeholders (especially those with a broad view of the economy)

Study questions

1 What are the technical and creative elements of event design, and how can they be evaluated?

2 For each of the main elements in sustainability planning indicate how social responsibility is to be evaluated.

3 Use three or more indicators of sustainability, financial viability and consumer relevance to assess the life-cycle of one or more periodic events or types of event.

Recommended additional readings and sources

Berridge, G. (2007). *Events Design and Experience*. Amsterdam: Butterworth-Heinemann.

Holmes, K., Hughes, M., Mair, J. and Carlsen, J (2015). *Events and Sustainability*. London: Routledge.

Jones, M. (2017). *Sustainable Event Management: A Practical Guide*, 2d.ed.. London: Earthscan.

Nonprofit Risk Management Center (https://www.nonprofitrisk.org/)

RiskWorld (http://www.riskworld.com/resources/)

10 Evaluating Visitors and Experiences

Learning objectives

- ☐ Know the various 'audiences' of events.
- ☐ Be able to make accurate attendance counts or reliable estimates.
- ☐ Be able to profile attendees according to: motivation and benefits desired; origins and trip type; activities and spending.
- ☐ Understand how to evaluate the cognitive, affective, behavioural, interpersonal and sensory components of event experiences – and the meanings of these terms.
- ☐ Be able to combine quantitative measures (the event experience scale) with qualitative (participant observation, ethnography, experience mapping).
- ☐ Learn how technological developments are providing new approaches and measures of event and tourism experiences.

10.1 Introduction

Understanding the visitors and their experiences is central to event studies, and the focus of considerable research effort. Evaluation contributes to theory development, but the focus here is on several important questions: is marketing effective? are we delivering the experiences and quality services we designed? how do our visitors evaluate us?

Here is the logic of the ensuing discussion. First, to know your visitors/audience requires data on attendance and a visitor description, plus information on motivation and benefits desired. How does this profile fit with marketing plans and target marketing? Second, how can the quality of visitor experiences be measured?

10.2 The audience

There are multiple audiences, stakeholders or constituencies for most events. Mackellar (2014) in the book *Event Audiences and Expectations* classified the audiences as:

♦ *Mass audience:* large crowds attending big events, often for hedonistic reasons; could include pilgrimage

♦ *Special interest*: the involved, attracted by event-specific benefits

♦ *Community:* events called 'community festivals' and the like, aiming to bring together members of specific places; could include fund raisers

♦ *Incidentals:* otherwise known as 'casual tourists', they attend because of general interest in the destination or someone takes them to the event

♦ *Media:* a mediated experience; social media now a dominant factor in experience co-creation

This typology can be related to the generic/targeted benefits dichotomy – discussed in the books *Event Studies* (Getz & Page, 2016), and *Event Tourism* (Getz, 2013) – which suggests that most event attendees are seeking generic leisure and social experiences, while those with special interests have different needs and expectations. Mackellar uses the term 'serious participation', based on Stebbins' theory on 'serious leisure' (Stebbins, 2006), and the sociological construct of 'social worlds' (Unruh, 1980). These theories sparked interest in examining the 'event tourist career trajectory' (Getz and McConnell, 2011) which has been applied to sport-event participants, food and wine tourists.

10.2.1 Attendance

Figure 10.1 lists some key evaluation questions, suggested KPIs and the data sources and methods available to evaluators. Note that for attendance the KPIs actually describe the measures needed for a comprehensive examination of attendance, and these data also contribute to other evaluation questions such as financial audits and economic impact assessment. The biggest challenge is always going to be the open-access event where crowd estimation is needed, and of course these can be exaggerated for political reasons. For a review of methods see Tyrrell & Ismail (2005) and Biaett and Hultsman (2015).

10.2.2 Profiling the visitor

Some events are not particularly concerned about target marketing and do not do segmentation studies, but for most events it is important to design experiences and services for the intended audience. Visitor profiles are therefore essential, and so is trend analysis to see if changes are as planned, or the event needs to adapt. Visitor surveys are the main source, but might have to be complemented by market area surveys. Observation can be used to gain a better understanding of the audience and their behaviour, but in some cases might be the only way to profile visitors. For an example see the research article by Katsoni and Vrondou (2017) that profiles sport event tourists.

Figure 10.1: The Evaluator's Toolbox: Attendance evaluation

Attendance: evaluation questions	Key performance indicators	Data sources / methods
Q-Are we reaching OR did we reach our targets (for total attendance; venue or programme attendance; ticket sales)? Q-Do we have a firm attendance count or a reliable estimate?	■ Total event attendance and at sub-events ■ Total number of guests, participants, or customers ■ Total number of visitations and ave. Visits per person/group ■ Turnover rate (# of new and departing visitors per hour) ■ Peak attendance ■ Ticket sales (combined with revenue per ticket this KPI can be more important than attendance)	■ Sales and revenue data ■ Turnstile counts (bodies through the gate) ■ Vehicle counts (also needed: ave. Persons per vehicle) ■ Crowd estimates (e.g., from police, photos, observation) ■ Market area surveys (usually by telephone) ■ Registration (often there are discrepancies between advance registration and actual attendance)

Figure 10.2: The Evaluator's Toolbox: Visitor profiles

Visitor profile: Evaluation questions	KPIs	Data sources & methods
■ Was our target marketing effective? (i.e., we attracted the anticipated segments) ■ Were there conflicts among visitor groups? ■ What are the trends in visitor types, and the implications?	■ Profile of each visitor 　■ Age in years 　■ Male or female 　■ Employment status 　■ Educational level 　■ Income level ■ Party type: family only; family and friends; friends only; alone; team or tour group ■ Size of party (number of visitors travelling together)	■ Visitor survey ■ Market area survey ■ Direct observation
Market area and trip type ■ Where did we draw visitors from? was this expected? what are the implications? ■ Travel data are needed for tourism impact assessments and carbon / ecological footprint analysis	■ Home address: country, state, city or town ■ Origin of trip on day of survey; distance travelled ■ Stops on the trip ■ Number and percent that are classified as tourists ■ Type of trip: accommodation used ■ Number of nights away from home and in the destination ■ Travel mode(s) (type of vehicle)	■ Visitor survey ■ Interviews with visitors ■ Visitor log books ■ Observation of vehicle origins ■ Traffic counts

10.2.3 Motivation and benefits sought

For practical purposes event organisers and tourism officials might only want to know the specific *motives* of visitors for their travel and attendance, and these can be expressed as desired activities (e.g., taste and drink, see exhibits, attend conference, compete), generic types of leisure experience (e.g., have fun with friends, family quality time, experience something new), or specific personal and social benefits desired (e.g., learn about heritage, health improvement, visit a specific site, city or venue, hear a particular speaker, listen to a favourite performer). But there are good reasons for digging deeper, to explore underlying motivation or need, and this introduces basic leisure and travel theory including Iso-Ahola's seeking-escaping theory (1980) and the differences between intrinsic and extrinsic motivation.

For impact assessment it is absolutely essential to question trip motivation. If economic benefits are to be attributed to an event it is necessary to determine that the event was the sole or main purpose of the trip. Otherwise, the visitor might be a 'casual' (already in the area) or a 'time switcher' (they would have come anyway, but at a different time). Asking about the 'percent importance' of the event in motivating the trip will provide the necessary information, with the range being from 100 percent to not at all. This should be combined with information on other reasons for the trip.

What people expect from travel or an event is of great interest theoretically, being tied to expectancy-confirmation theory, and it is an important element in measuring satisfaction or using importance-performance measures. When we get to a discussion of quality this will be re-visited.

For more sophisticated understanding of motivation, involvement scales and behavioural measures can be employed to determine the level of involvement with any leisure, sport or lifestyle pursuit. The Mackellar (2014) book on event audiences is a good general reference.

Figure 10.3: The Evaluator's Toolbox: Motivation and benefits sought

Motivation & benefits sought: Evaluation questions	KPIs	Data sources and methods
■ What are the underlying motivations and the specific benefits sought? Do they fit with our design and marketing? ■ What reasons are given for trips to the area and attendance at the event?	■ Percent importance of the event in motivating the trip; other trip reasons ■ Expected experiences, ■ Activities, goods and services ■ Previous trips and attendance at event ■ Involvement level (in sport, leisure or lifestyle pursuits)	■ Pre-event survey ■ Visitor survey at the event ■ Post-event follow-up ■ Interviews

10.2.4 Visitor activities and spending

Some of these data are needed for financial analysis and for economic impact assessment. Visitors can be observed, and asked what they did, but innovative methods are also available, such as GPS tracking. There have been many studies of event and event-tourist activities and spending, for example by Anderson (2017), who examined both reported spending and intent to spend.

Figure 10.4: The Evaluator's Toolbox: Activities and spending

Activities and spending: evaluation questions	KPIs	Data sources and methods

▪ Do visitors behave as expected?
▪ What interests them the most?
▪ What are their on-site movements and schedules?
▪ Can we forecast and measure actual visitor and tourist expenditure attributable to the event
	▪ Attendance at specific event activities or venues
	▪ Activities on the trip and elsewhere in host community
	▪ Spending on:
	  ▪ Travel (car etc.)
	  ▪ Accommodation
	  ▪ Purchased meals
	  ▪ Groceries
	  ▪ Entertainment, other events, attractions
	  ▪ Other shopping
		▪ Visitor survey
		▪ Turnstile count
		▪ Ticket sales
		▪ Observation
		▪ Business survey in the area
		▪ Financial records of the event and suppliers
		▪ Systematic observation (including photography, video, GPS tracking)

10.3 Experience evaluation

The event and tourism experience is not merely about behaviour (i.e., activity and spending), it also has to be understood in terms of cognition (thinking) and emotion. Behaviour can be observed, but the other two experiential dimensions cannot. So what can the evaluator do to understand event experiences? With constant improvements in technology, especially the use of various wearable devices, it is becoming much easier to get experiential data at events, but that should complement and not replace qualitative methods. This section provides a review of available methods and measures, with clear implications for event planning, design and marketing.

Berridge (2007) in *Events Design and Experience*, advocates a symbolic interaction approach to design and evaluation, based on the work of Rossman (2003). This framework examines the six elements of interacting people, relationships, rules, objects, physical setting and animation. The first consideration is to profile the audience and consider their desired benefits and expectations, then how they interact with each other both physically in terms of symbolic meaning. For example, audiences at live music concerts can behave in ways that confirm social identity (we are part of this group) and reflect (sub)cultural norms like singing along, participating in a mosh pit, drinking or drug taking. Symbolism also has to be considered in the location and design of the setting and how the event is managed, as there are accepted and expected ways of doing things for different social or cultural groups. It should also be remembered that events can be 'iconic' (possessing high symbolic value) within social worlds because they are viewed in certain ways such as the biggest, best, most challenging, or most popular with the highly involved.

Pearce and Zare (2017) advocated an 'orchestra model' as the basis of tourism experience design, consisting of the three traditional experiential components (affective, cognitive, behavioural) plus relationships and sensory components. Their recommended design tools are also valuable as evaluation tools. Figure 10.5 provides their list, plus annotations provided by this book's author as a contribution to the evaluator's toolbox. Some of these tools are elaborated upon elsewhere in this book, but it can be seen that some of these have as yet unrealized potential.

Figure 10.5: The Evaluator's Toolbox: Experience design and evaluation tools

Experience design tools (Source: Pearce and Zare, 2017)	Applications
Stakeholder maps: "Necessary coverage of the participants: A listing and possibly a spatial representation of all the personnel or likely sets of actors involved in the experience space."	Stakeholder mapping is fully examined in the companion book *Event Stakeholders*. Getz & Page (2016: 245) in *Event Studies* examine the experiences of different event stakeholders.
Systematic observation: "Observations to be recorded include the visible elements of the orchestra model- sensations, activities, time spent and the range of relationships."	Has been applied in service mapping (see chapter 11). See also checklists, participant observation (e.g. Berridge, 2014), and ethnographic research including the Shipway case study.
Contextual interviews: "Directly assessing the views of the actors. "	The experiences and satisfaction of athletes, performers, staff, volunteers, suppliers and other actors has to be evaluated. Alonso (2016) did in-depth interviews with businesses collaborating in a gastronomic event.
Photo elicitation: "The researchers provide participants with cameras or encourage them to use smart phones to photograph the important parts of the experience."	Davies et al. (2015) used participant-led photography to explore experiences. An alternative is to show photos to visitors or potential consumers regarding how people react to, or prefer environments and experiences. *Foodies and Food Tourists* (Getz et al., 2014) and the article by Andersson et al. (2016) examine photo elicitation in detail in the context of determining what food tourists prefer – the answer is hands-on learning events! Park et al., 2010 combined photography with participant observation to evaluate an event.
Service staging/Role plays: "The physical acting out of scenarios and prototypes by the student/group to model the customers' existing or new experience."	Can this technique be integrated with focus groups, in addition to design workshops? Use direct observation of activity at events as an input. See the Beard case study in Chapter 11.

Netnography: "Researchers access comments made by visitors on major online evaluation sites (e.g. Trip Advisor) or review the content of online blogs and forums. Both text and photo analysis of these resources can be used.	Systematic analysis of online content, mostly on blogs, has been used by Getz and Patterson (2013) to explore various social worlds and their event-tourism links. As people get more involved in a hobby, leisure or lifestyle pursuit planned vents tend to become more important, leading to event travel careers.
Cognitive mapping: "...ask participants to draw a sketch map of their visit highlighting points of interest and the recalled layout of the setting."	Can be combined with service mapping, GPS tracking of event visitors, identification of hot and cold spots, and evaluation of visitor interactions with people, setting and management systems. Lask (2011) used cognitive mapping as part of event impact assessment.
Storyboards: "A series of drawings or pictures that can be used to portray a sequence of involvement with a space. Can be used to plan new situations or reflect on existing practice."	The storyboard can assist in creating a logic model for goal-attainment evaluation. A possible application is to ask visitors, in interviews, to draw pictures of their experience – combine this with service mapping.
Desktop models and simulations: "Small scale three dimensional models can be used to layout the full setting which actors experience... If available, computer programmes with three dimensional images can be used as similar tools for exploring change possibilities. "	Simulations are at the frontier of design and evaluation. As a formative evaluation tool, a computer simulation or 3D model could reveal problem areas and enhancement opportunities. Could be combined with wearable biometrics to test reaction to entertainment or other programming features. Arcodia (2002) discussed simulation gaming and Fotiadis & Sigala (2015) described an actual game.
Service blueprints/Co-creation: "A close detailed specification of each point in the service encounter... Co-creation involves accessing the views of actual participants in contributing to creative ideas to improve the occasion."	Combining blueprinting and service mapping (see Chapter 11) with direct customer feedback.
Narratives: "Communicating design ideas through a strong narrative is a method for sharing and convincing others of the value of change and innovation."	Narratives should be related to storytelling, myth making and interpretation as experiential facilitators. Ask participants and customers to tell their stories!
Personas/Market segments: "A group by group identification of the experiences offered by the new design features.."	Segmentation of the audiences can be combined with experience evaluation before and after events.

10.3.1 Participant observation

Pettersson and Getz (2009) documented a research project that combined participant observation and photography with visitor interviews and a post-event survey at a major sporting event (World Cup Alpine Skiing, in Are, Sweden). The research identified *hot and cold spots* within the host village and event venues, these being defined by the presence or absence of attributes to hold a visitor's attention. Use of GPS was suggested as an additional tool to obtain a complete picture of movements and time allocation during the event visit.

Research note

Pettersson, R. & Getz, D. (2009). Event experiences in time and space: A study of visitors to the 2007 World Alpine Ski Championships in Åre, Sweden. *Scandinavian Journal of Hospitality and Tourism*, **9**(2-3), 308-326.

Abstract: The spatial and temporal nature of event experiences was studied through interviews, participant observation and photography at a major sporting event. Results contribute to a better understanding of how visitors interact with the event setting and with each other, and help build theory on experiences, their design and management. Event tourists were observed spatially and temporally while enjoying various elements of the host village and four event arenas, while photographs and notes made by participant observers enabled a more focused evaluation of positive and negative experiences. Results identified the importance of social factors, as visitors wanted to be where the others were, revealed that surprise created positive experiences, and identified the existence of experiential 'hot spots' defined in both time and space. It is concluded that positive experiences are more important than negative ones in terms of overall satisfaction. Implications are drawn regarding the nature of event experiences, their design and management, and on related methodological development.

Key words: Event experiences, design, management, temporal/spatial patterns

10.3.2 Using technology

Brown and Hutton (2013) examined technological and methodological methods for evaluating on-site event behaviour (see the research note). They argued that common research and evaluation methods pertaining to experience can be supplemented through monitoring devices that can measure changes in heart rate (e.g., in response to programming or crowding), measure motion and time intervals, measure calories, and detect unsafe body conditions (perhaps indicating the need for medical treatment).

Research note

Brown, S. & Hutton, A. (2013). Developments in the real-time evaluation of audience behaviour at planned events. *International Journal of Event and Festival Management*, **4**(1), 43-55.

Abstract: The purpose of this paper is to explore recent technological and methodological developments in the evaluation of audience behaviour at planned events and discuss the implications for researchers in this field, particularly the advantages of evaluating in real-time. The creation and staging of the event experience – the realm of event design – is predicated on an understanding of the psychosocial domain of the audience. By understanding the motivations, behaviours and predispositions that the audience brings to the event, and how event design principles and techniques can be applied to influence audience behaviour in real time, the event designer is able to more successfully create and stage the event experience to meet the aims and objectives of the event.

10.3.3 Survey methods and an experience scale

In an effort to gain a better understanding of event experiences, and to provide a standard evaluation tool, De Geus et al. (2016) developed a scale for visitor surveys. It was based on leisure theory and standard ways of measuring leisure experiences, encompassing behaviour, cognition and affect or emotion. They describe *affective engagement* as consisting of excitement, emotional energy, adventure, values and recollection; *cognitive engagement* as encompassing interpretation, learning, intellect, knowledge acquisition, and reflexivity; and *physical engagement* relates to activity, creativity and multisensory experiences. Their research led to the addition of a fourth dimension called *experiencing novelty* which fits with the notion of events as 'extraordinary experiences' from Morgan (2008).

Actionable research was undertaken by Peperkamp et al. (2015), this being evaluation of festival experiences with a view to enhancing event design. They used participant observation to describe the 'visitor journey' before, during and after festivals in Rotterdam, and this is similar to the approach needed for service mapping and blueprinting. They concluded (p. 145.) "The visitor journey approach, which included participant observation research in combination with the creative session, was positively received by representatives from both the event organisations and the Rotterdam Festival partners, first because it succeeded in changing stakeholders' perspectives from supply-side thinking to visitor centred thinking. As one of the event directors expressed it: 'the visitor journey challenges you to take on the role of the visitor and provides you with surprising new insights'." Conclusions also identified four main design challenges:

"(1) Creating basic vs. memorable or transformative experiences;

(2) Providing a convincing event story to the visitor vs. allowing and stimulating each visitor to construct his or her own story;

(3) Passive event consumption vs. active event consumption, and

(4) Focusing on direct-experience vs. focusing on all phases of the experience."

Research note

Peperkamp,E., Rooijackers, M. & Remmers, G-J. (2015).Evaluating and designing for experiential value: The use of visitor journeys. *Journal of Policy Research in Tourism, Leisure and Events*, **7**(2), 134-149.

Abstract: Evaluation and monitoring have become major issues for cultural events. On the one hand, more detailed information is needed to satisfy event sponsors, on the other hand, the nature of events is increasingly developing towards inclusive concepts (from consumer-oriented delivery to more experiential and social values). The focus on visitor experience presents event organisers with a need to go beyond traditional measurement instruments to evaluate their events. Qualitative approaches are therefore increasingly valued for the insight they provide into visitor experience. The use of visitor journeys and thematic analysis for evaluating, monitoring and improving cultural events will be discussed on the basis of research in cooperation with Rotterdam Festivals, an umbrella organisation for festivals in the city of Rotterdam.

Another potentially useful research and evaluation method is 'human experience mapping' as described by Beard and Russ (2017). See the research note below and the case study by Colin Beard in the next chapter.

Research note

Beard, C. & Russ, W. (2017). Event evaluation and design: human experience
    mapping. *Event Management*, **21**, 365-374.

Abstract: This article reports a phenomenological evaluation of a small-scale cause-related event. Three complimentary methods were applied to the interpretation of data obtained from interviewing participants who took part in an event involving the experience of sleeping on the streets with homeless people in a city in the UK. The participant experience data were first explored by applying a simple multiphasic interpretation. A second layer of exploration involved separating the data into six human experience dimensions. A third and final interpretation method involved the collaborative construction of a schematic map as a composite-summative expression of the data.

10.4 Case study: Using participant observation as an evaluative method at events and festivals

by Richard Shipway (Bournemouth University)

The three most common qualitative research methods are participant observation, in-depth interviews, and focus groups. Participant observation is appropriate for collecting data on naturally occurring behaviours in their usual contexts, and this case study highlights how its use offers unparalleled insight into the social world of the event participant. Participant observation is the act of looking at the setting and people in detail and over time, systematically studying what goes on and noting and reporting. It is an inductive approach that has origins in anthropology and sociology and from the early periods of fieldwork, when researchers such as Malinowski (1922) and Mead (1935) became part of the culture they studied, and examined the actions and interactions of people 'in the field'. As such, event researchers as participant observers would look at people and events in their natural settings.

Prolonged engagement and involvement is one significant characteristic of participant observation, and is needed to learn about the event setting and people being studied. Whilst observation is considered less disruptive and more unobtrusive than interviews, participant observation does not just involve watching, but also listening and talking to the event participants being studied, and it can be conducted in open and closed event settings. An open setting will be public and highly visible, such as within the crowd at a major sporting event, while in closed settings access is difficult; backstage at a music festival could be considered as a closed setting. The participant-observer enters the setting without intending to limit the observations to particular people or situations and adopts an unstructured approach. Certain ideas might emerge in the early stages, but usually observation progresses from being unstructured to the more detailed and focused, until specific actions become the main interest of the researcher. Researchers can then observe social processes as they happen and develop, and situations can be analysed. There are various types of observer involvement in the field. These are the complete participant; the participant as observer; the observer as participant; and the complete observer (Holloway and Wheeler, 2010), and these sometimes overlap and boundaries become blurred. When participant observation is successful, it uncovers interesting patterns and developments that are grounded in the real world of the event participants' daily lives.

The observation of a variety of contexts within an event setting is important. Spradley (1980) states that participant observation takes place in social situations, and provides a framework in order to guide researchers. In Figure 10.6 Spradley's framework for participant observation is applied in an event / festival context. Using the annual New York City Marathon as a point of illustration allows the reader to grasp the applicability of the technique for event studies. The framework could be used as a template for the study of any event or festival. Through using an inductive approach to research, the focus of observation will inevitably change in response to the data generated as the research proceeds.

Figure 10.6: Participating in the New York City Marathon: adapted from Spradley (1980: 78)

New York City Marathon

Space: The Festival location, e.g. the New York City Marathon and the surrounding streets of the five NY boroughs that the course passes through.

Actor: The person in the Festival setting, e.g. the runners, the security personnel, the police officers, the on course spectators.

Activity: The behaviour and actions of those in attendance in New York, e.g. running, supporting, volunteering.

Object: The items located in the setting, e.g. runners clothing, event barriers, supporters signs and banners.

Act: The single action, e.g. policing 26.2 miles of NYC, crowd cheering and support.

Events: What is happening (in the period post, during and pre)? e.g. the context and importance of the Marathon to New York, or proposed event impacts and legacies of distance running events.

Time: Timeframe and sequencing, e.g. media build-up (traditional press and online), planning and organisation activities leading up to the main race day (Race Expo, Saturday Breakfast Run), post-event activities such as clean up operations.

Goal: What participants are aiming to achieve, e.g. (depending on actor role) raising awareness, minimising disruption, fun and enjoyment, profiling NYC as a tourist destination.

Feeling: The emotions of participants, e.g. accessible through observation on the days; the press in the build-up to race day; and the atmosphere on the course.

Spradley (1980) suggests that observers take three main steps: they use *descriptive*, *focused*, and finally *selective* observation. Descriptive observation incorporates general ideas that the observer has in mind, and everything taking place in the situation becomes a source of data and should be recorded, including smells, colours or appearances of people present. Description involves all five senses (Holloway and Wheeler, 2010). As time progresses, certain important aspects or areas of the event setting should become more obvious, and the researcher will be able to focus on these. Finally, the observation will become highly selective. To aid data collection, it is suggested that event researchers utilise the observation guidelines provided by LeCompte et al. (1993), detailed below in Figure 10.7, which will be particularly useful when starting field research, when feelings of being overwhelmed by the task ahead exist.

Figure 10.7: Observational guidelines for events and festivals

1. The **'who'** questions: Who and how many people were present in the event or festival setting or taking part in activities and events. What were their characteristics and roles within the environment?

2. The **'what'** questions: What is happening in the setting, what are the actions and rules of behaviour of those present? What are the variations in the behaviour observed?

3. The **'where'** questions: Where do interactions between event attendees take place? Where are they located in the physical space of the setting?

4. The **'when'** questions: When do conversations and interactions take place? What is the timing of the activities or actions; and do discussions and interactions take place at different times.

5. The **'why'** questions: Why do attendees in the setting act the way they do? Why are there variations in behaviour?

Shipway et al. (2016) combined participant observation and semi-structured interviews to gain a better understanding of the event experiences of active sport participants at the Tour Down Under (TDU), a professional cycling race event held in Adelaide, South Australia. Cycle tourists were observed during the event at a range of locations including the start and finish lines of each stage, the Tour Village (the hub of the event), out on the race route at selected strategic race points, and other cycling events held in Adelaide during the event week such as criteriums and social events. The event researchers were also able to observe and interview participants in a range of outdoor event spaces such as bars, cafes or grassed areas.

Through the use of participant observation and subsequent interviews three main themes emerged from the data: first, the interaction of people and temporary spaces on a cycle event tourism 'stage'; second, the co-creation of authentic personal experiences and meanings; and third, identity reinforcement and the development of a sense of belonging. Consequently, a model for understanding sport event tourism experiences was developed (Shipway et al.,

2016). Observations during the six day cycling event, described by participants as a 'Festival of the Wheel', indicated that providing event tourists with authentic and memorable experiences were central to the event experience and that the cycling events provided individuals with a sense of belonging or membership to a wider social group. The key elements of the event experience, obtained through the use of participant observation and interviews, are illustrated in Figure 10.8.

Figure 10.8: Key elements of the event experience

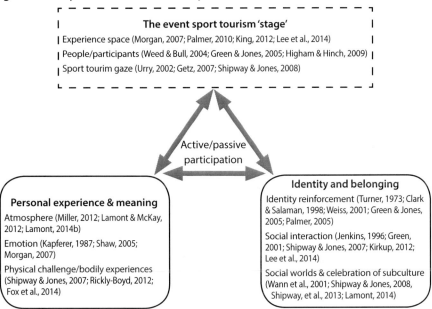

In summary, the need to understand underlying experiences, feelings and emotions related to event behaviour have resulted in qualitative research taking on increasing importance within events studies. This case study, through the use of examples from the sports events context, illustrates that the strength of participant observation as a form of qualitative research is the ability to lift the veil on certain aspects of a chosen event and to make visible unknown cultural aspects.

Study questions

1 Construct a template for profiling and segmenting visitors or other event audiences, including discussion of how the data are to be collected and analysed.

2 Describe a triangulation approach (at least three methods) for evaluating the visitor experience at a specific type of event (e.g., sport event, convention, festival). Consider at least two different segments or audiences.

Recommended additional readings and sources

Mackellar, J. (2014). *Event Audiences and Expectations*. Abingdon: Routledge.

11 Quality Evaluation

Learning objectives

☐ Define 'service quality' in marketing terms, but be able to explain the important differences between event programme and service quality and how they can be measured.

☐ Learn the SERVQUAL approach and the five gaps model and how they can be adapted to event evaluation (e.g., FESTPERF).

☐ Be able to measure satisfaction augmented by importance-performance measures.

☐ Understand the principles of service blueprinting and mapping and their usefulness for experience design and quality control.

11.1 How people evaluate service quality

Knowing how visitors evaluate programme and service quality is crucial for marketing and design, and for continuous improvement of the co-created event and tourism experience. It goes beyond the visitor, as Derrett (2015:333) described various stakeholder perceptions of festival quality, demonstrating how it means different things depending on one's interests and goals. The attendees, organisers, suppliers, government, grant givers, sponsors, the public (non users) all should be evaluated – especially when determining overall worth. But even when examining service quality, there might very well be big differences in what stakeholders find to be important and in their evaluation of performance or quality.

The evaluation of service quality is a big topic in the marketing, tourism and events literature, with several theoretical foundations being relevant. The classic articles by Parasuraman et al. (1985, 1988) set the tone and remain essential reading. Regarding leisure and events, Mackay and Crompton (1988) examined "search, experience and credence" factors that pertain to customer evaluation of quality. Note that in this context, programme and service quality are not separated – the event or the tourism experience IS the service.

Search: When searching opportunities, such as attending events, there are certain tangibles that can be identified, and information found, that might affect the decision to attend or influence expectations. These will include the location and site, programme, organisations and people participating, cost, and services available. Importance-performance evaluation will reveal what was considered to be most important, although the method cannot cover every possible consideration. Pre-evaluation, such as through focus groups and searching media accounts of the event, will help in formulating a comprehensive list of factors to include and these can be refined through experience or by examining what was found at other events.

Experiences: You cannot know in advance what experiences you will have at an event, although expectations will usually exist for a level of quality. These are in part shaped by reputation, social media interactions, and marketing. Special evaluation methods are required to explore experiences, although many evaluators simply ask about satisfaction with programme and service quality.

Credence factors: Customers might be unable or unwilling to evaluate the professionalism or technical competence of people and equipment they encounter. This applies to artists and athletes as well, although people can report on what they like. Event evaluators will use some input from customers, but additional expert opinion and the feedback of peers will be needed to assess competence.

Equity: Applied to public services, such as government supported events, and probably the not-for-profit sector's events, many people will consider equity principles in their evaluation of quality. While the private sector seeks profits, and sometimes produces events unaffordable to large segments of the population, there is little or no justification for government events and service-oriented events to exclude people on the basis of price. On the other hand, if events are free or easily affordable the attendees might very well modify their expectations of quality, be less demanding and critical. This remains an hypothesis to test!

Figure 11.1: Visitor experiences and satisfaction

Recommended goals for visitor experiences and satisfaction	Sample KPIs
■ Understand the experiences desired and realized by guests	■ High satisfaction on all highly important elements using importance-performance analysis
■ Satisfy our visitors with the event overall, and with all elements of programme and service quality	■ Zero or reduced complaints
■ Determine ways to improve the event	■ High level of recommendations by word of mouth
■ Determine future intentions (loyalty) and the likelihood of word of mouth recommendations	■ Increasing or high level of return visits and expressed loyalty

11.2 Measuring quality: SERVQUAL

There are two measurement models in widespread use: one simply asks about customer satisfaction with service attributes, and the other compares expectations with perceived performance to identify discrepancies (as in the Importance-Performance method). The discrepancy model, including I-P measures, generates more information with multiple potential uses. Both approaches have their supporters and critics.

Regarding why visitors attend, the underlying theory for SERQUAL and Importance-Performance measures is 'expectation-confirmation'.

From Wikipedia: *"Expectation confirmation theory is a cognitive theory which seeks to explain post-purchase or post-adoption satisfaction as a function of expectations, perceived performance, and disconfirmation of beliefs."*

The popular SERVQUAL discrepancy-based model by Parasuraman, Zeithaml and Berry (1988) consists of five distinct dimensions to measure consumers' expectations and perceptions of service performance: tangibles, reliability, responsiveness, assurance, and empathy. Each of these give rise to evaluation questions that can be included in visitor surveys or interviews, with analysis augmented by service mapping or less systematic observation.

Figure 11.2: SERVQUAL Dimensions

SERVQUAL Dimensions (Source: Parasuraman et al., 1988) **and recommended goals**	Suggested KPIs for events and event tourism
TANGIBLES ■ Ensure that all tangible aspects of the event site (design, appearance of personnel, and visitor services like toilets, food, parking, comfort, merchandise) are of the highest possible standard ■ Ensure accessibility is adequate for all visitors ■ Reduce or eliminate waiting times	■ Zero deviations from specifications ■ High customer satisfaction
RELIABILITY ■ Get everything right (to specifications) and accurate the first time ■ Honour our promises (as communicated in media and signage) ■ Visitors must have confidence in the organisation (it is reassuring when there are problems), the schedule (produce the event on time) and delivery of what was promised (i.e., the programme) ■ Ensure that patrons understand different levels of service provided (related to price, location or time) ■ Treat all visitors as honoured guests	■ Zero complaints and/or all complaints dealt with immediately and to the customers' satisfaction ■ Zero departures from the published schedule and programme ■ Satisfaction with responses to service failure ■ High degree of trust among stakeholders
RESPONSIVENESS ■ Staff and volunteers will always be prompt, and willing to help, when responding to requests and solving problems ■ Empower staff and volunteers to "go the extra mile" in delivering quality services and satisfying customer needs	■ High customer satisfaction with recovery from service failures ■ High satisfaction on staff/volunteer helpfulness and on information provision ■ Satisfaction of staff and volunteer (self-assessment) ■ Supervisor satisfaction with workforce

ASSURANCE ■ All guests will feel safe and be confident in our security measures ■ Staff and volunteers will always be polite, competent and trustworthy ■ Our reputation will be constantly enhanced through quality events and service ■ Be proactive in communicating with and listening to customers and other stakeholders	■ Complete satisfaction with perceived safety and staff/volunteer competence ■ Zero incidence of staff/volunteer misbehaviour ■ High reputation relative to other organisations/events (measured with stakeholder feedback and media analysis)
EMPATHY ■ Our stakeholders and customers will always be made to feel like honoured guests and individuals with needs ■ The health/safety, convenience and experience of attendees will be of paramount importance ■ Ensure that visitor needs are understood by the organisation and staff ■ Workers will provide individualized attention	■ High satisfaction with perceived hospitality, friendliness, convenience, comfort, helpfulness ■ Increased loyalty and word of mouth recommendations

Research note

Park, M., Daniels, M. J., Brayley, R., & Harmon, L. K. (2010). An analysis of service provision and visitor impacts using participant observation and photographic documentation: The National Cherry Blossom Festival. *Event Management*, **14**(2), 167-182.

Abstract: Using participant observation and photographic documentation, a study of the National Cherry Blossom Festival was conducted to evaluate service provision and impacts on National Mall and Memorial Parks (National Mall) resources. Specifically, the researchers examined the adequacies of National Park Service facilities and services to meet festival visitors' needs as well as assessed human impacts on the natural and cultural resources in the National Mall. The study results suggested that the nature of this cultural event led to intense, concentrated consumption and usage of facilities, services, and natural resources, making it difficult for management to keep up with visitor demand and risking long-term degradation of the natural resources.

11.2.1 Five-Gaps Model

The Five-Gaps model (Parasuraman et al, 1985) provides additional perspectives on quality, with the evaluator looking for specific sources of service failure and the reasons.

Figure 11.3: The Evaluator's Toolbox: Five-Gaps model

The Five-Gaps model	Evaluation challenges
Gap 1 occurs when event managers or tourism marketers do not understand customer needs, motives and expectations, so the design or marketing campaign is wrong.	Evaluators provide evidence that is used in planning and design to meet the needs, motives and expectations of target segments.
Gap 2 occurs when management does not translate its perceptions of customer needs and expectations into design and service specifications.	The use of logic models and service blueprinting is intended to prevent this mistake.
Gap 3 is the difference between specifications and what actual gets done, and the possible reasons for this are many.	Evaluators have to look at how specifications are communicated, staff and volunteer training and attitudes, and any other factor influencing actual service delivery.
Gap 4 pertains to the marketing of events and tourism, whereby wrong impressions might inadvertently be given, inadequate information disseminated, or just plain exaggeration and misrepresentation	Marketing and communications have to match the actual experience and level of service offered. Evaluate both real and perceived gaps, as people sometimes do not fully understand or pay close attention to information.
Gap 5 is the measure of discrepancy between customer expectation and perceived quality.	Importance-performance deals explicitly with this gap, whereas satisfaction measures are also used as a summary of customer perceptions. When problems are identified use the root-cause methods previously described.

11.3 Importance-Performance evaluation

This is an important tool with many possible applications. Here we look at I-P in the context of evaluating guest or customer expectations and satisfaction, yielding much more information than a simple "are you satisfied with…" type of question. The downside is that you need more information and therefore time from your guests.

There are two somewhat different applications. The first concerns why people came to the event (motives and expectations) and whether or not they got what they expected. This helps explain overall satisfaction and aids in strategic planning. The second is more focused, examining specific elements (or attributes) of programme and service quality and getting performance ratings for each.

People come to an event expecting certain things, possibly no more than a different kind of experience. But the expectations of experienced event goers will evolve, even if they are going to new events. And many loyal visitors will probably expect more and better every time. By asking about what was important in motivating their visit or trip, underlying needs and motivations are revealed. The difference between what they expect and their evaluation of performance is called 'disconfirmation of beliefs' and can be positive or negative.

Figure 11.4: The Evaluator's Toolbox: Importance-Performance Evaluation

Importance-Performance evaluation	Technique: Sample questions
Importance can relate to WHY an event was chosen OR the relative importance of specific attributes in determining overall satisfaction.	■ "What attributes of the event were important to you when deciding to attend this event?" (list attributes and leave space for respondents to write more) ■ "What attributes of the event were important in determining your overall satisfaction or dissatisfaction with this event"? list attributes and leave space for more
The performance (or satisfaction) questions apply to all the attributes listed or identified by respondents. An alternative is to rate the perceived quality of each attribute and the event overall.	■ "What is your level of satisfaction with these attributes of the event"? OR " What is your assessment of the quality of each of these attributes?"

Here are examples of how to develop the questions and measurement scales:

◆ For **Importance**: "Not at all important, somewhat important, somewhat unimportant, completely unimportant" OR add a neutral point and use a 1-5 scale.

◆ For **Satisfaction**: "completely unsatisfied, somewhat unsatisfied, somewhat satisfied, completely satisfied" (again, a neutral point can be added)

◆ For **Quality**: "very bad, poor, good, excellent" or similar terms; OR use a 1-10 scale with ten being "excellent" or "perfect".

The mean values (i.e. averages) are calculated for all responses to both scales, and this forms the dividing line on the grid. When you plot the scores you might see a skewing towards one or the other of the four quadrants, which might reflect respondent bias (people tend to avoid being overly critical), so if the results are not informative in separating the attributes, try changing the grid lines. This can be done by placing the grid lines where the top twenty or top ten percent of scores fall into the top-right or top-left quadrant. The idea is to isolate those items that are of high importance and of low quality or satisfaction, relative to the others, then decide how to improve them. As well, you want to isolate attributes of quality that are both important and that you are doing well. Mean scores close to the grid lines might be hard to interpret, which is another reason for looking at results when the grid lines are moved (see Figure 11.5).

If you use IP to examine motives versus performance, there are implications for marketing. For example, if the feature or attribute 'excellent food and wine' was very important to many people, but quality/satisfaction was low, then perhaps the communications were misleading. Note that 'hygiene factors' do not attract people but can disappoint them. Also, event-goers can be critical of many elements but still be satisfied and intend to return! That is why the IP analysis should be supplemented with an overall satisfaction question like "Overall, how satisfied were you with your event experience?"

More refined analysis of IP can compare responses on demographics, motivational segments, involvement, or repeat versus first-time visitors. Statistically, you might also look at the standard deviations for each score.

Figure 11.5: Importance-Performance illustration

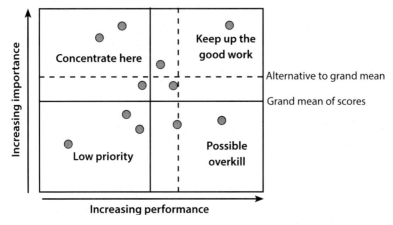

Research note

Smith, S., and Costello, C. (2009). Culinary tourism: Satisfaction with a culinary event utilizing importance-performance grid analysis. *Journal of Vacation Marketing, 15* (2), 99–110.

Abstract: The aim of this research was to provide a practical method for assessing satisfaction at a culinary event. Twenty-seven culinary event attributes items were analyzed from an international culinary event. MANOVA was employed to identify differences between importance and performance measures. Importance-performance analysis (IPA) was subsequently used to assist culinary event organisers while identifying critical performance attributes in order to improve customer satisfaction. Findings revealed food and beverage prices, come/go, convenient parking, and food tasting had high importance scores, yet low performance measures. The use of multiple regression analysis confirmed three out of the four attribute items had a predictive effect on overall satisfaction.

11.4 Service blueprinting and mapping

The 'service blueprint' lays out specifications for providing services at an event according to a specific framework, while the 'service map' is an evaluation tool that uses the same frame. They can be combined, or the mapping/evaluation can be done first, leading to recommendations for improving service. A combination of methods can be used, such as secret shoppers or participant observation, checklist observation, self-reporting by staff and volunteers, and visitor feedback. It is rather time-consuming and complex and has been used infrequently in the event and tourism fields.

Figure 11.5: The Evaluator's Toolbox: The service map

The Service Map	Technique
1: Map the visitor's entire experience (a simpler alternative is to concentrate on just one activity, venue or programme)	1) Imagine, or from experience re-create, the entire process and actions taken by visitors to enter, experience, and depart from the event. ■ This will likely have to be subdivided into specific venues and programme elements that each require their own blueprint. ■ Consider how visitors will interact with others, the setting, staff and volunteers, suppliers, and your management systems. ■ Goals can be derived from the Logic Model, which sets up the evaluation process that includes service mapping.
2: Specify required and likely customer-staff interactions	Describe the nature, location and timing of all planned and possible encounters with staff and volunteers; which ones are crucial for logistics and for quality experiences? ■ This is sometimes called the 'front stage' as staff and volunteers are both service providers and contributors to the visitor experience; they have to be trained in how to perform their tasks and respond to incidents; performers and competitors for spectator events are part of the front stage.
Tangible evidence	Describe all possible tangible evidence of services provided, that is everything the visitor sees and comes into contact with that affects their satisfaction including information, hygiene (e.g. toilets), comfort stations, food and beverages, décor, merchandise, uniforms, entertainment, the sport or competition, learning opportunities, etc.
Management systems and operations	Specify all management systems and operations necessary to achieve the event's goals and maximize visitor safety, health and enjoyment (i.e., an operations and logistics plan). ■ This is the 'back stage', invisible to the visitor, such as supply, hidden logistical systems, security, communications, etc. It can also be called the 'infrastructure' and is often provided in whole or in part by the venue. Various other systems have to be in place to facilitate the event, such as marketing and communications, fundraising, and office administration.

The categories in both blueprinting and mapping are the same. They start with the premise that the visitor experience can be broken down into discrete actions and settings, which of course does not get at the true nature of leisure experience. Relating the specifications to SERVQUAL and Five-Gap dimensions will help the evaluator and event designer. A Logic Model will help, but only in general terms. More appropriate will be 'story-boarding', a technique for visualizing how visitors will be experiencing the event, in sequence.

Research note

Getz, D., O'Neill, M. & Carlsen, J. (2001). Service quality evaluation at events through service mapping. *Journal of Travel Research*, **39**, 380-390.

Abstract: Service mapping is described and illustrated in the context of evaluating and improving service quality at special events. Results of participant observation at the 1998 Margaret River Masters surfing event in Western Australia are combined with concurrent visitor survey data and direct observations to generate recommendations for improving its management. Conclusions are drawn on the utility and application of the service-mapping technique for events and on the nature of service quality at events.

Here is a summary of the evaluation process followed at the surfing event, with the intent being to obtain customer feedback and create a service map leading to recommendations for event improvements.

1 Planning: The team set evaluation goals and detailed the method, based on consultations with the event manager and knowledge of the event itself. Ethical permission was received, and the logistics agreed with the manger.

2 Team training involved design of observation checklists, visitor surveys, and agreement on how to conduct participant observation.

3 Assigning individual evaluators to the event by time and place.

4 At the event each observer completed their own checklists, obtained survey completions, and wrote in a log book. These are the elements observed, with comments written on the effectiveness of services and perceived quality or service failure:

♦ Approach and arrival (e.g., traffic, signs noted, staff directions)
♦ Parking (conditions, ease of access)
♦ Entering the site (queues, instructions, confusion)
♦ Seeking information (sources, clarity)
♦ Buying and consuming food and beverages; souvenirs (cost, quality, availability)
♦ Observing the event (seating, views)
♦ Departing

Interactions with staff or volunteers. Evaluators were asked to comment on how each encounter affected their experience and to evaluate the effectiveness of the staff/ volunteers. For example, were the evaluators annoyed, pleased, or left unsatisfied?

♦ Asking directions or for information
♦ Receiving instructions
♦ Observing their appearance and behaviour

Observations on other tangible evidence of service, including:

♦ Brochures, tickets, or other material received before and during
♦ The physical appearance of all aspects of the site
♦ The programme (e.g., running on time, knowing what was happening)
♦ Security and crowd control measures and their effectiveness
♦ Pedestrian flow on site (congestion? confusion?)
♦ Crowd behaviour (rowdy? quiet? noisy? dirty?)

5 Completion of the log book after the event, and analysis of all data. Observations and comments from log books were combined with data from checklists and visitor surveys to prepare the service map.

11. 5 Evaluation of crowd management and control

'Crowd management' refers to all the design and management systems aimed at visitors to ensure a safe and rewarding experience, while 'crowd control' refers to actions taken when there is a need for policing, emergency response, or other direct interference with event visitors. Evaluation starts with the usual attention to logistics and operations, customer experiences and satisfaction, and critical incidents. See Silvers' (2008) book on risk management for details.

Figure 11.6: Crowd management and control

Recommended goals for crowd management & control	Sample KPIs
■ Ensure the safe, orderly and comfortable movement of people and vehicles ■ Meet all fire & safety regulations; ensure continuous compliance ■ Make improvements based on evaluation of crowd behaviour ■ Train all personnel in emergency responses ■ Work with police, health services & security to monitor crowd conditions and be able to prevent or react effectively to incidents ■ Provide state of the art communications facilities and networks to ensure that necessary information is always available ■ Set venue and site capacity limits to ensure safe, comfortable and pleasing crowd limits ■ Avoid any action or design feature that could lead to panic, sudden movement and crushes ■ Enforce rules and regulations regarding alcohol, drugs, firearms or other dangerous substances	■ Positive visitor and staff/volunteer perceptions of crowding and crowd management ■ Reduced line-up times (or avoid altogether) ■ Reduced or zero serious incidents and health issues ■ Effectiveness of safety and security as measured by feedback from personnel and customers

Case study: Experience mapping

By Professor Colin Beard, Sheffield Business School, Sheffield Hallam University

When a higher education student conducted a small scale piece of research on the experiences of women from HSBC bank who had slept out on the streets of Sheffield (UK) for just one night as part of a wider charity project to increase awareness of the plight of homeless people, I found the results particular interesting. However the student found the massive amount of raw data he had collected hard to interpret.

In order to help the student understand this data I first of all asked him to disaggregate it into a number of dimensions of the human experience, such as their emotional experiences, their sensorial experience, anything associated with knowing and knowledge, etc. He covered the following: (1) knowing, (2) doing, (3) sensing, (4) feeling, (5 & 6) belonging (people and places) and (7) being (identity etc).

The student now had two forms of data. The first one was the data from his original interview questions, whilst the second batch represented the same data allocated to one seven dimensions of the human experience. The second phase, which was quite easy to complete, helped the student considerably in his interpretive work, yet he was still struggling.

What concerned me was the fact that traditional academic data, presented in this way to the inexperienced eye, proved difficult to comprehend. This was made worse by the fact that many columns of written words were printed out on several sheets of paper. This format of data linearity is difficult for the human brain to comprehend and to detect 'patterns'.

I was determined to develop an approach that would allow both the student and future event industry practitioners to more readily grasp large bodies of data collected in a traditional (academic) way. What I was looking for was a method that would simply and quickly create a rich picture of the sleep-out experience.

What evolved was a clear sequence that converted the original chronological or multiphasic academic questionnaire, firstly into a view of data as disaggregated into several human experiential dimensions. This was then followed by a spatial-relational, mapping approach that generated quite a rich picture of understanding in a relatively short time. This experience mapping process was later tested out with many professionals around the world with considerable success. The experience mapping method involved three to five people gathering around a long roll of paper three or four metres long and one metre wide, divided in to three sections to denote the periods before, during and after the sleep out event. They read the original data, as handouts, from the first two approaches and they were simply encouraged to scribble down anything that they found of interest. People were initially overwhelmed with the six to seven pages of data and so they sometimes got stuck: they had to be pushed to just get on with writing *something*. This was an important step in building confidence.

After about 30 minutes people were asked to have a dress rehearsal of their understanding of the participant experiences. They had to walk alongside their scribbles talking about what they had so far. Everyone contributed to the emerging narrative. This led to a period of further development when all groups felt they wanted to have more understanding and intentionally looked to fill in gaps as they saw them or more complete interpretations. During the final collaborative 'walk the talk', completed in front of peers, the narrative even gained greater complexity, taking on a higher cognitive level of critical analysis. The resulting discussion, and the generation of a rich picture of the event experiences was quite astonishing. The mapping processes has subsequently been carried out successfully in Hong Kong, Singapore, USA, Malaysia, Slovakia and the Czech Republic.

Mapping and talking and sharing appears to have been key to this final process. Brain research shows that linear formats limit the capacity to identify spatial-relational connections. London taxi drivers appear to have enlarged areas of the hippocampus due to their work in comprehending and navigating the spatial layout of thousands of roads and streets. The process here is not dissimilar to the mapping processes that Harry Beck used to create the London Underground map that is now replicated around the world to depict transport system complexity in a simple manner. Is experience mapping a process that can be refined and used more readily by event practitioners to critically explore and evaluate participant experiences?

Questions asked:

1. What was your relationship with the charity like before the event?
2. Do you regularly donate time or money to charities in general and if so what kind?
3. What motivated you to attend the event?
4. What did you want to get out of it?
5. Have you attended other events like this for charity?
6. Tell me about your experience during the event?
7. Which of your senses were stimulated the most? (hear, see, touch, smell)
8. What emotions arose during and after the event? (think/feel)
9. What was the most engaging part of the experience?
10. Did the experience bring the participants closer together?
11. Do you feel you are more part of a CAP community because of this?
12. After the event, how has your relationship/ view of the charity and awareness of the cause changed because of the event?
13. Have you talked positively about the experience and charity with your friends, family and colleagues since the event?
14. How much involvement/contact with the charity have you had since the event and why?
15. How has your view on homelessness changed because of the event?
16. Would you now choose to donate to CAP over other homeless charities and why?
17. How does it compare with a regular charity event (gala dinner/concert/fair)?
18. Is there anything else you would like to add about how the event affected you?
19. What did you think of the interview overall? What was good about it? And what could be improved?
20. Other unplanned responses and questions

Study questions

1. Design a survey to conduct an Importance-Performance evaluation of a real event. Test it on a small sample of attendees. Derive recommendations for improvement.

2. Interview one or more event managers to obtain their expert opinions on their event's quality. Use the five-gaps model and ask questions specific to all the SERVQUAL elements. Discuss improvements with the managers.

3. Pick a real-world event for participant observation and prepare a service map that can be used to recommend improvements. Alternatively, prepare a detailed service blueprint for a new event. Both can be done as a team project.

Recommended additional readings and sources

Silvers, J. (2008). *Risk Management for Meetings and Events*. Amsterdam: Elsevier

Wikipedia article on SERVQUAL: https://en.wikipedia.org/wiki/SERVQUAL

12 Evaluating Human Resources

12.1 Introduction

Events often face difficult challenges in human-resource management, as discussed in books by Van der Wagen (2007), Baum (2006) Baum et al. (2009) and in Handbook chapters by Hanlon and Jago (2012) and Schlenker et al. (2012). Each challenge has implications for evaluation, and here are some of the big ones.

♦ Experiences are at the core, and workers (visible and off-stage) are part of the experience co-creation process; how can we evaluate that contribution?

♦ Risks are plentiful, and the unexpected might occur, placing workers in a difficult position; working conditions vary greatly, both indoors and outdoors, sometimes in crowded spaces, and workers might be isolated.

♦ Volunteers are usually essential, and often are the dominant service delivery group. How are they to be evaluated relative to paid employees? Do they have their own motives and ways of evaluating their satisfaction?

♦ Professionalism in event management is not a universal constant (Where is education/training? Who certifies professionals? What code of ethics applies?)

♦ Incentives, rewards and pay are often not in line with government and the private sector, making recruitment, motivation and retention more difficult;

can self-evaluation and teamwork contribute to higher levels of satisfaction and performance?

◆ Pulsating events might have only a few permanent staff, with periodic recruitment and training bursts as the event nears; how do we measure training effectiveness in that context?

Specific HR risks or problems to look for, as discussed by Van der Wagen (2007:31), include the following.

◆ Mismanagement: owing to poor recruitment or training? there is a constant need for a crisis management team and contingency plans to cope with failures and mistakes.

◆ Staff shortages (due to a failure to recruit as planned, or to dissatisfaction of staff and volunteers?); events must have a back-up recruitment plan.

◆ Loss of key personnel, leaving a gap to be filled by recruitment or sharing duties within teams.

◆ Attrition during the event: is there a need for better working conditions or rewards? Re-deployment might work, but only if cross-training has occurred.

◆ Misconduct, resulting in conflicts or negative media coverage; suggests a need for counselling and for discipline or dismissal options.

◆ Critical incidents occur to which workers must respond, and workers might be the victims. Is training for incidents adequate? Crisis response teams have to be in place.

12.2 HR planning and management evaluation tasks

Lynn Van der Wagen in the book *Human Resource Management for Events* (2007), covered the main steps in the process, starting with workforce planning. At each stage, from start to wind-up, evaluators have a key role to play. The figure provides suggested goals that actually define the process, and KPIs for evaluators.

Figure 12.1: Human resources planning and management, goals and KPIs

Suggested goals for HP planning & management	Sample KPIs
Planning ■ Establish HR policies and procedures; integrate with overall planning and project management ■ Conduct and periodically revise job analysis and job descriptions ■ Determine the roles of paid staff, volunteers and teams ■ Develop a recruitment, induction, training and motivation plan ■ Establish, testing and refine performance evaluation methods and measures	■ All positions filled with competent personnel ■ Managers' reports on sufficiency of staff and volunteer workers (numbers and competence) ■ Regular performance measures Efficiency measures: ■ Reduced cost of recruitment and training ■ High levels of commitment and retention

Organisational design	■ Worker evaluation of management systems and managers
■ Building the organisation so that staff and volunteers are placed appropriately, supervised, and evaluated	■ Visitor and stakeholder evaluation of the event's staff, volunteers and service quality
■ Blending and/or separating paid staff and volunteers in terms of motivation, tasks, evaluation criteria	
■ Internal evaluation plus getting feedback from relevant external stakeholders	
Recruitment and training	■ All positions filled according to schedule
■ Recruitment and training to be completed on schedule	■ Reduce or eliminate worker problems, complaints, disciplinary actions
■ Disciplinary action or termination, if warranted	■ Zero or reduced accidents and injuries
■ Evaluating effectiveness of recruitment and training (with real-time adjustments as necessary)	■ Immediate attention to work environment issues
■ Risk, health and safety	
■ Standards and regulations to be implemented and checked	
■ Assignment of responsibilities for risk assessment, critical incident response and reporting, and evaluation/ correction procedures	
Wrap-up	■ Post-event evaluation of the workforce by management and stakeholders
■ Stakeholder consultations/feedback	■ Post-event evaluation by staff and volunteers
■ Summative evaluation, especially considering retention	■ Improvement of effectiveness and efficiency measures over time
■ Report on HR evaluation; recommendations for continuous improvement	

12.3 Motivation, satisfaction & commitment

Barron and Rihova (2011:207) reviewed the literature and theory on volunteer motivation, as applied to planned events, concluding that: "The diversity of the research findings suggests that there is not one generic response to the issue of volunteer motivation. It differs depending on the nature of the volunteering activity, the context in which it is measured, and the demographics of the target group." There is little doubt that the type of event influences who volunteers and why, as social and professional affiliations and leisure interests lead many into volunteering.

Motivational theory (discussed in Van der Wagen, 2007) is a useful starting point for evaluation, mainly because if you understand what motivates people you are more likely to employ the most relevant criteria and methods, and then achieve higher levels of performance, satisfaction and commitment. For example, volunteers seeking a learning opportunity to prepare for a career (this is common for students) or to network as part of a job search, might be more amenable to positive feedback on how to improve their general work skills than those who seek specific benefits from events like meeting people, or tangible rewards such as tickets and parties.

As part of recruitment, or subsequently, volunteers should be asked about their motivation and goals, as a way to understand their needs and to place and supervise them correctly. This question gets to the importance of generic reasons for volunteering, and can be augmented by adding event-specific questions (e.g., pertaining to the entertainment, the sport, the location, the organisers).

In general, volunteer motivation can stem from values, such as doing good (i.e., altruism), self development (acquiring skills) hedonism (having fun, socialising) or a utilitarian perspective (extrinsic motivators like the promise of rewards).

Figure 12.2: The Evaluator's Toolbox: Measuring volunteer motivation

Measuring volunteer motivation	Technique
Altruism	Q: To what extent do you agree or disagree with these statements? (use a 1-7 scale, from completely disagree to completely agree) ■ I want to give back to my community ■ I feel good about volunteering ■ It is all worthwhile when I really help the guests ■ It is my civic duty to help out with this event
Promise of reward (extrinsic motivation)	■ Free tickets are a good incentive to work at the event ■ They have great parties / have lots of fun ■ I was told I have to volunteer (by school, church, club, a judge, etc.) ■ To advance within the organisation I have to volunteer
Leisure	■ This event appeals to me because of my interest in this sport/leisure activity/hobby ■ It is something I do to be part of a group; all my friends are volunteers here ■ It's a lot of fun
Self-development:	■ This will give me useful training ■ I find it challenging and satisfying to do good work ■ It is to my advantage to network and meet new people ■ I need the experience before getting a paying / better job

Through surveys, interviews or observation, sources of dissatisfaction can be detected. Commitment to the event or organisation is in part behavioural (how long do volunteers and employees stay?) and part attitudinal. Understanding motivations and dissatisfaction are starting points. The elements of commitment can include personal or social identification with the event, organisation or a cause.

Figure 12.3: The Evaluator's Toolbox: Dissatisfaction and commitment

Dissatisfaction & committment	Technique
Sources and degree of dissatisfaction	Q: To what extent do you agree or disagree with these statements? (use a 1-7 scale, from completely disagree to completely agree)
	■ We are subjected to poor working conditions (e.g., long hours, bad/inadequate food; danger; noise; isolation; physical strain; emotional stress)
	■ I feel overworked / burnt out
	■ There is a lack of proper training
	■ I cannot realistically do the job assigned because I do not have the skills or knowledge
	■ The organisation does not adequately recognize or reward my effort
	■ I am not being used in the best way
	■ I am competent to take more responsibility
	■ I am bored; there's nothing for me to do
	■ Our / My supervisor is – mean/incompetent/ uncaring
Attitudinal measures of commitment	Q: To what extent do you agree or disagree with these statements? (use a 1-7 scale, from completely disagree to completely agree)
	■ I believe in the purpose and goals of this event
	■ My needs for enjoyable and rewarding work are met by the organisation.
	■ I plan to continue working for the event for as long as possible.

12.4   Evaluating training effectiveness

The Kirkpatrick (2007) hierarchical model can be adapted to different evaluation tasks, such as training effectiveness or ROI, ROO and ROE measures for events (discussed in Chapter 13). Evaluators are cautioned to start at the bottom and not try to determine ROI or long-term impacts before measuring reaction, learning and behaviour. Figure 12.4 illustrates this approach and Figure 12.5 provides details pertinent to events. Note that it cannot be expected that training, learning and behavioural improvements will automatically lead to a better event for attendees, or success for organisers.

At the base, level 1, is *reaction,* or what the trainees feel and say about their experiences. If the training sessions are boring, poorly designed or intimidating, the effect might be negative. They have to be asked in a way that encourages honesty and thoroughness, as well as conveys the intent that managers need and will use as feedback to improve. Immediate and longer-term feedback from trainees is essential. Do trainees think they learned enough? Was the training programme useful to them, and were the trainers effective and approachable? Subsequently, did the training prove adequate to do the job and provide skills to respond to new demands or unexpected incidents?

Figure 12.4: A hierarchical model for evaluating training effectiveness. Adapted from Kirkpatrick and Kirkpatrick, 2007

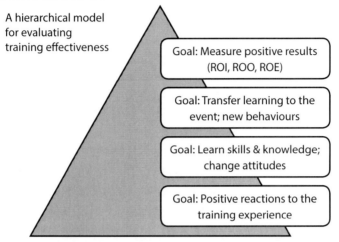

A hierarchical model for evaluating training effectiveness

Goal: Measure positive results (ROI, ROO, ROE)

Goal: Transfer learning to the event; new behaviours

Goal: Learn skills & knowledge; change attitudes

Goal: Positive reactions to the training experience

The checklist or survey can be similar to the evaluation forms used by meeting planners in evaluating presenters and corporate or academic training sessions.

♦ The place: suitable, comfortable, convenient

♦ The trainers: competence, approachability, friendliness

♦ The delivery: adequacy of AV, online/computer/tablet, printed material

♦ Clarity of goals, objectives, for each person or team

♦ Clarity of job description or team roles

♦ Clarity regarding the evaluation process as applied to staff/volunteers

♦ Suitable or customized to particular needs? (e.g., disability, gender, race, learning style)

♦ Followed by on-site or experiential training

♦ Rating scale for degree of satisfaction

Trainees should also be able to provide useful suggestions for improvements. This might be combined with an evaluation of emotional response during and after training sessions, including direct observation of participants, a post-event wrap-up session with open discussion of how participants felt, or even a survey asking about the following:

♦ How did you feel during the sessions? (e.g., agitated, uncomfortable, excited, bored)

♦ When the sessions were over, how did you feel? (e.g., disappointed, exhausted, relieved, happy, eager)

Figure 12.5: Evaluation of training effectiveness, goals and KPIs

Recommended goals for evaluation of training effectiveness	Sample KPIs
Base Level 1: Trainees will find the experience to be beneficial, enjoyable, and transforming.	■ High satisfaction levels ■ Emotional response ■ Recommendations for improvement
Level 2: Trainees will demonstrate competence in the required skills and knowledge.	■ Pre and post-tests to demonstrate increased knowledge and skills ■ Supervisor feedback on actual practice
Level 3: 'Graduates' of training will demonstrate on-the-job behaviour that reflects increased knowledge, skill, commitment and productivity	■ Behaviourally anchored rating scales can be used
Level 4: Staff and volunteers will be recognized by visitors and other stakeholders as being a positive force in co-creating a satisfying and memorable experience for all concerned. ■ Overall customer/guest/stakeholder satisfaction will increase through effective training programmes ■ Fewer problems experienced among staff and volunteers and attributable to them	■ High levels of stakeholder satisfaction with the event and specifically with staff and volunteers ■ High(er) satisfaction and commitment levels of staff and volunteers ■ Decrease in complaints and problems related to staff/volunteers

Level 2 concerns the measurement of learning, such as through knowledge and skill testing during and after an event. An unavoidable problem that must be taken into account is memory loss and the potential need for reinforcement.

Level 3 is 'behavioural changes', and these will be challenging to evaluate. The aim is to demonstrate that learning/training does change the behaviour of staff and volunteers. They will have to self-report on this, combined with observation and supervisor reports (see HR evaluation methods). Customer and stakeholder feedback will also be important.

'Business impact' is level 4, and is focused on how training/learning directly affects job performance, such as reducing customer complaints or saving money because of efficiency gains. This is a typical aim of corporations producing meetings and training sessions, but in the case of events the desired impact is different. Assuming the intent is to improve the event, and the training focuses on event staff and volunteers, then the business impacts will be reflected in such metrics as fewer accidents, higher customer satisfaction, and hopefully improved staff/volunteer morale and commitment. In the long run, effective training will be a key to success and sustainability.

At the top of the pyramid is ROI, normally expressed in monetary terms like profitability or return on assets. For events, the Return on Objectives/Goals approach will usually be more relevant. It should not be expected (and it would be almost impossible to prove) that training effectiveness leads to a more successful or sustainable event. On the other hand, without it no event producer can be confident in the future.

12.5 Performance evaluation

Because staff and volunteers are often crucial to quality visitor experiences and to overall event success, evaluating their performance is critical. It is not a once-in-a-while task, indeed a permanent performance evaluation system is needed. A comprehensive performance management system incorporates evaluation at all stages: formative, process and summative.

Figure 12.6: HR performance management goals and KPIs

Recommended goals for HR performance management	Sample KPIs
Develop and communicate clear policies and procedures for performance management and evaluation.	▪ High levels of knowledge and acceptance of policies and procedures
Work with managers, stakeholders, staff & volunteers to develop acceptable and effective performance standards and measures, tied to job analysis and job descriptions. ▪ Methods are to be adapted as appropriate to changing circumstances	▪ No discrepancies between job descriptions and performance measures
Employ multiple and reinforcing methods of performance evaluation, (for example: 360° evaluations within teams and functional areas, self-appraisals, supervisor reports, and critical incident reports).	▪ High degree of acceptance: review effectiveness and worker acceptance of each performance method and measure
Provide the training, rewards and support necessary to ensure workers feel confident, fulfill their duties, and remain satisfied.	▪ Knowledge and skills tests ▪ Availability of on-site support staff ▪ High levels (or improvement in) satisfaction, commitment and loyalty
Enforce standards sympathetically and with a view to continuous improvement, utilizing discipline and termination as a last resort.	▪ Reduced (or zero) rate of terminations owing to disciplinary action or underperformance

12.5.1 Management by objectives

Management by objectives was popularized by Peter Drucker in his 1954 book *The Practice of Management*. It is part of human resource management, but of course the objectives have to come down from overall organisational strategy and goals. Not only does the setting of clear objectives drive HR activity, it shapes evaluation and presumably leads to a more productive workplace. Staff and volunteers are evaluated on their performance according to standards. When staff and volunteers are part of the process of setting objectives and standards (or performance measures) it is believed they will be happier and more effective.

One potential problem with MBO is that workers might lose incentive to go beyond their agreed-upon tasks and will become slaves to the performance measurement system. This could impede innovation and even lead to a poor service environment. Critics point out that leadership, based on systems thinking, is a better way to motivate workers.

12.5.2 Teamwork and quality circles

Although generally considered to be a rejected fad from the 1980s, the quality circle could find a home in event teamwork where collaboration and inclusion are valued. The basic idea is to ensure that quality is implemented throughout the process, not just to evaluate outcomes and try to correct problems. In this way it is a potential tool for implementing the Balanced Scorecard or Event Compass. The evaluation is continuous, and is the responsibility of teams.

Basu and Wright, in *Quality Beyond Six Sigma* (2003), specified seven conditions for successful implementation of quality circles. These are summarized below:

1 Quality circles must be staffed entirely by volunteers.

2 Each participant should be representative of a different functional activity.

3 The problem to be addressed by the QC should be chosen by the *circle*, not by management, and the choice honoured even if it does not visibly lead to a management goal.

4 Management must be supportive of the circle and fund it appropriately even when requests are trivial and the expenditure is difficult to envision as helping toward real solutions.

5 Circle members must receive appropriate training in problem solving.

6 The circle must choose its own leader from within its own members.

7 Management should appoint a manager as the mentor of the team, charged with helping members of the circle achieve their objectives; but this person must not manage the QC.

12.5.3 360 degree evaluations

In this approach, everybody evaluates everybody else – at least within their work group or area of responsibility. If it is not customized to the work setting, however, things can go seriously wrong. In some event personnel situations the crucial evaluators should be guests or customers, not other staff or volunteers. And if everyone evaluates supervisors and the CEO, are they being fair? Do they really know what is going on? Length of time in the position will often determine the validity and completeness of 360 ° evaluations for the obvious reason that exposure over time yields insights – but it can also generate inter-personal recriminations.

12.5.4 Rating scales

Rating scales have many applications in evaluation, particularly in performance evaluation of staff and volunteers. See the website (http://www.performance-appraisal.com/ratings.htm) for useful advice. One overall consideration is that the use of standardized scales allows for direct comparisons among people/situations and over time.

Scales are unlikely to account for all possible scenarios. For example, some staff or volunteers might be expected to work in extremely stressful, customer-oriented situations, while most do not – should they all be evaluated on the same scale items? Some flexibility and customization will therefore usually be necessary. Also, no scale can account for all success or failure factors, and it is wise to remember that individuals can excel in one area and not in others. Accordingly, supervisors and teams need to get workers into jobs where they can make their best contribution.

Ranking employees or volunteers against each other, using the same criteria, can be difficult and time consuming in large events. Staff and volunteers can also rank each other anonymously, but unless there are clear patterns the results might be suspect. In paired comparisons each person is ranked against every other in the group, on the same criteria.

Figure 12.6 illustrates a number of approaches. Context is important, as is the testing and refinement of scales to yield the best information for decision-making. The question of how many items are to be in the scale is less important than the utility of the ratings – that is, can evaluators validly distinguish between satisfactory and unsatisfactory, or exceptional and normal? The purpose of MBO is to make it clear how the individual is to be evaluated, but that still leaves the important question of whether the scale allows for valid comparisons across all staff and volunteers.

Scales can cover multiple domains; the contexts and sample scales in the Toolbox can be combined.

Figure 12.7: Evaluator's Toolbox: Rating scales in performance evaluation

Performance evaluation	Sample rating scales
Management by objectives The focus is on objectives set for individuals through negotiation, so that the person being evaluated knows the criteria in advance	1 Unsatisfactory: does not meet their personal objectives 2 Below expectations; meets some but not all their objectives 3 Satisfactory: performance is in accordance with their objectives 4 Above expectations: meets all objectives and goes beyond 5 Exceptional performance; exhibits leadership, innovation, unexpected talent
Comparative performance The evaluator compares individuals across a type of job or within a team; the points of comparison should be known in advance, such as: does punctuality matter? is everyone expected to do the same thing in the same way, or is variance tolerated?	1 Unacceptable: consistently performs below expectations and is demonstrably less effective/consistent/punctual than the others in this team or job category 2 Acceptable: meets the requirements set for this job or team as well as all the others 3 Exceptional: meets and goes beyond all requirements for the team or job category, performing better than most others

Team performance Here the team is responsible for its overall performance within an MBO context and individuals are not separately evaluated; the team must take internal action to maximise performance; teams can be compared with others, or evaluated solely with regard to their assigned function.	1 The team does not achieve its objectives 2 The team meets all its objectives 3 The team meets all its objectives & demonstrates excellence, innovation or superb performance
Competency The evaluator is testing or using indicators of competency to do a specific job; this could also be applied to teams.	1 Unacceptable: does not demonstrate the required skills or knowledge 2 Acceptable: demonstrates all require skills and knowledge 3 Exceptional: demonstrates superior knowledge and skills, exceeding all requirements
Behaviour In some circumstances the behaviours of staff/volunteers are most important; can be combined with other scales. (see the ensuing discussion on BARS):	1 Demonstrates unacceptable behaviour (e.g., Not punctual; does not meet dress code; fails to answer questions) 2 Consistently demonstrates some effective behaviours, but not others 3 Always demonstrates acceptable behaviour 4 Often demonstrates exceptional behaviour; serves as a role model and mentor
Self-reporting In some circumstances it might be necessary to rely upon self-reporting; in others, this could complement other forms of evaluation; can be done in very simple terms, as in the example opposite, or on a numeric scale. An alternative would be to self-evaluate on a complete set of competencies and/or behaviours.	1 I have weaknesses or failures that I would like to correct (name them) 2 I am doing a good job, meeting all my objectives (perhaps offer evidence) 3 I am outperforming others and feel I have exceptional ability (but what is the implication - do they want a promotion? greater reward? re-assignment?)

Behaviourally anchored rating scales (BARS) are popular, with the person being reviewed already assumed to have a job description. The evaluator, often a supervisor, determines whether or not the person has fulfilled their specified duties. These can also be done by self completion, as part of a learning process (i.e., becoming the reflective professional intent on continuous improvement).

BARS pertain to a number of dimensions of work:

♦ Quantity: e.g., the person did everything they were supposed to; volume of people processed; numbers of items sold.

♦ Quality: e.g., how well they did their work; possibly a reflection of how they are valued by other staff/volunteers; possibly using customer/guest feedback; no errors.

♦ Timeliness: e.g., were they slow, fast, on time? compared to others?

◆ Process: e.g., the correct steps were taken, if specified.

◆ Outcomes: the desired outcomes are sometimes intangibles, like customer satisfaction or high-quality performance, in which case additional input is required.

12.6 Critical incidents: characteristics, response and reporting

Disaster! Crisis! These terms describe what it usually means to experience a 'critical incident' at an event. But 'critical' can also refer to turning points, as in an incident that becomes a catalyst for change. In the marketing literature they speak of 'moments of truth' when a customer interacts with personnel, venue, programme or a management system (like the event website or a platform for mobile devices) and then forms an opinion or makes a decision that can alter their attitude and behaviour in good or bad ways – from finding the event boring or too pricy, leading to complaints or bad talk, to having a WOW experience and becoming loyal fans.

Figure 12.8: The Evaluator's Toolbox: Sample critical incident report

Facts	Response
Time and place of incident:	**Name and position of reporter:** **Witnesses (staff and others):**
Nature of the incident; type and severity of injury etc. Possible or obvious causes	▪ What was immediately done and by whom? ▪ Follow-up: removal to hospital? Called police or fire?
Was the incident recorded? Was there mass/social-media coverage?	▪ Checked for media accounts? ▪ Are photos, videos available?
Outcomes for those affected (might require a time delay)	Outcomes for the event/organisation ▪ Legal ▪ Financial ▪ Reputational ▪ Other
Follow-up	Evaluation and recommendations ▪ Change procedures, plans or policies? ▪ Training? ▪ Physical alterations to site, etc.? ▪ Insurance needed? ▪ Advice needed?

Critical incidents are also experienced by staff and volunteers and can be the basis of evaluation. In this method the evaluator (a supervisor usually) reviews incidents with the person being evaluated, hopefully in a positive manner that leads to improvement. The incident data can come from log books kept by supervisors or staff/volunteers, or derive from customer complaints or praise.

The response to, and evaluation of critical incidents is essential to prevention and continuous improvement of the event. While the first responders are going to be on-site staff and volunteers, they must be prepared for any number of contingencies, starting with the high probability of accidents and illness. At many events staff and volunteers will have immediate backup from professional health workers (e.g., St. John's Ambulance) and from police and/or security personnel.

The critical incident report provides, alongside eye-witness accounts, detailed information for later analysis.

Study questions

1   Reflect on your own career motivation and find appropriate theory in the literature (e.g., as discussed in the book *Event Studies*, Getz, 2012) to provide insights; what does the theory say are the important differences between employees and volunteers?

2   Use the Kirkpatrick model to examine your own student or professional education/training. Where has it been strong or lacking? What would you recommend for improvement?

3   What kind of performance evaluation would you like to have applied to your work? Compare different approaches and give your reasons. As a supplementary task, design a rating scale for the kind of work you do (or have done).

4   Discuss critical incidents from the perspectives of customer, worker and supervisor. What is the evaluator's role in each of these cases? Give examples of incidents.

Recommended additional readings and sources

Kirkpatrick, D.L., & Kirkpatrick, J.D. (2007). *Implementing the Four Levels*, Berrett-Koehler Publishers.

Basu, R., and Wright, J. (2003). *Quality Beyond Six Sigma*. London: Elsevier.

Van Der Wagen, L. (2007). *Human Resource Management for Events*. Amsterdam: Butterworth-Heinemann.

13 Evaluation in Different Types of Planned Events

Learning objectives

☐ Understand that different types of events present their own unique evaluation challenges.

☐ Be able to determine the motives, decision criteria, expectations, and satisfaction of attendees at business events

☐ Be able to measure return on investment, return on objectives, return on experience and conversion rates

☐ Be aware of special evaluation issues and challenges regarding festivals and cultural celebrations

☐ Understand methods for judging artistic quality

☐ Know the motivational and behavioural differences between sport participants and spectators, and what this means for evaluation

13.1 Introduction

Each type of planned event offers different experiences, often in special-purpose venues, and therefor presents unique challenges for the evaluator. Events have different *forms* (i.e., what they look like, their inherent characteristics) and functions (i.e., what they are intended to do, their goals and impacts). Every event is unique in some way, related to the combination of programme, setting, people, and management.

In this chapter three major categories of planned event are examined, namely business events, festivals and cultural celebrations (including special attention to the arts), and sport.

13.2 Business events

Figure 13.1 is a starting point for looking at different types of business event and related evaluation challenges. Charity events and private functions are included here for convenience.

Figure 13.1: Business events, private functions, and key evaluation challenges

	Some key evaluation challenges
Business events ■Meetings, Conventions, Congresses ■Fairs, Exhibitions (Trade and Consumer shows) ■Corporate Events ■Fund Raisers (charity) ■Educational & Scientific	■Determining the motivations for attending when it is optional ■What criteria and process should be employed to find the best location and venue? ■Evaluating the experience from different perspectives ■What is the quantifiable ROI? For corporations and associations, suppliers and exhibitors, and attendees; how do cities gain real value from investing in venues, marketing and bidding? ■Operationalising return on experience and return on objectives ■What are the ethical issues in fund-raising? ■Can 'live event' or 'experiential' marketing be fun? Is it intrusive? ■What is the source of competitive advantage in these markets?
Private functions ■Rites of passage (e.g., birthdays, Bar Mitzvahs) ■Parties ■Reunions ■Weddings	■Details of service quality can be of paramount importance in satisfying clients ■Is the client always right? When do professionals put ethics and standards above client satisfaction?

13.2.1 Meetings, conventions and congresses

Meetings are one of the most common forms of planned events. They are found in just about every business and organisation. They range from small ones that people have to attend, and are often routine in the office, to major international congresses. Professional meeting planners aim to make them useful, cost and time-effective for clients, and more attractive, memorable, and satisfying to attendees. For the evaluator a necessary starting point is with the standards, advice, and education offered to members of professional associations.

The evaluator should have comprehensive knowledge of meeting planning and operations. In the book *The Business and Management of Conventions* (McCabe et al., 2000) major concerns are discussed: the business environment; stakeholders; supply; bidding; human resources; site and venue selection and design; housing; marketing; operations; quality management and evaluation; finances; legal and ethics. More recent books stress social media and technology. When in doubt, start with established specifications or standards.

Specifications

The Convention Industry Council produces the *APEX Event Specifications Guide Template* (www.conventionindustry.org) and this is a useful starting point for evaluators. Checklists are provided, making compliance or fulfilment the main evaluation task.

This is a four-part document:

"Part I: The Narrative – general overview of the event.

Part II: Function Schedule – timetable outlining all functions that compose the event.

Part IIIa: Function Set-up Order – specifications for each function that is part of the overall event (each function of the event will have its own Function Set-up Order).

Part IIIb: Function Set-up Order (Exhibitor Version) – specifications for each booth/stand that is part of an exhibition"

Motivation to attend; decision factors

Understanding why people travel to corporate and association meetings and conventions, and their decision-making process, are major topics in the literature. Meeting and exhibition planners want to optimize attendance, with purpose and venue capacity in mind, and this means attracting specific target segments. Several associations combined to conduct the 'Decision to Attend Study for Conventions and Exhibitions' (The Experience Institute, 2017) with a major finding being that attendees are ever-more discerning travellers motivated by education (95% of respondents), the destination (78%) and networking (76%). About half either want to extend their stay or bring someone with them on event trips – logically, meeting and exhibition planners need to partner with destination marketing organisations! As always, cost and time constraints remain the main barriers.

Return on Investment, Objectives and Experiences (ROI, ROO and ROE)

Effectiveness can refer to something simple like attracting a financially viable number of attendees, or knowledge retention on the part of participants – it is largely context-specific. Three measures (ROI, ROO, ROE) are being used, although return on investment is the dominant term. ROI might be important to a company wanting to motivate its employees and increase their commitment, innovation or productivity, in which case they want to know the impacts on profitability or some other metric linked to competitiveness.

ROO (Return on Objectives - or goals) does not necessarily require monetary measures, it can include satisfaction, self-reported learning outcomes, attendance growth, etc. Evaluators have to follow a logic model to determine if goals are met, and also if they are appropriate.

ROE (Return on Experience) is the most challenging evaluation task of the three. ROE recognizes that experiences are co-created and so the organisers are providing a 'service proposition' that the attendee might or might not buy into. Meetings and conventions that add experiential components outside the venue are trying to make the overall experience more unique and memorable with the intent of increasing satisfaction, loyalty, positive word of mouth and, ultimately effectiveness from the point of view of whoever is paying.

To evaluate ROE requires new methods, perhaps starting with phenomenology by getting attendees talking about their actual experiences and how they feel about them. Were events engaging, unique and memorable is one thing, but what does that have to do with the aims of the meeting or convention organisers? Participant observation will help the evaluator understand the context. If companies and associations want event experiences to fuel organisational change or improve ROI, then a longer-term perspective will be needed to assess what experiences are shaping commitment, innovation or productivity. Figure 8.2 includes a number of recommended goals for meetings and conventions and a sample of linked KPIs.

Figure 13.2: Goals and KPIs for meetings, conventions and congresses

Recommended goals: meetings, conventions, congresses	Sample KPIs
Set and attain realistic attendance targets.	▪ High conversion rate (details follow) ▪ Attendee profile (should match targets) ▪ Zero no-shows (those registered but failed to attend)
Make information and registration processes user-friendly and problem-free.	▪ Zero or reduced complaints ▪ Positive feedback from attendees
Engage attendees before, during and after the event to maximize satisfaction, effectiveness (related to specific goals) and loyalty.	▪ Engagement discerned through social media content analysis (using the event or organisation's accounts) ▪ Satisfaction measured in post-event attendee feedback ▪ Learning and behaviour change as measured through pre and post-event testing (use the Kirkpatrick model)
Maximise ROI, ROO and ROE (for the owner or client).	Appropriate KPIs might include the following, requiring follow-up surveys and testing: ▪ Knowledge retained and skills learned (leading to cost reductions, changes in productivity, or quality improvements) ▪ Changes in attitudes and organisational culture ▪ Increased satisfaction, commitment and loyalty leading to better retention of staff or volunteers ▪ Innovations; enhanced creativity ▪ Stronger networking or better working relationships among people ▪ Sales and revenue increases (this is often the aim of having motivational speakers)

Conversion rate

This is a form of ratio analysis to measure both effectiveness in getting a desired result, and efficiency (considering effort or cost). For online activity evaluation requires statistics about site visits or contacts (e.g. how many visits, how many persons receiving information) and subsequent action (e.g., re-tweeting, liking, sharing, buying). Other uses require information from attendees or travellers about their activities or future intentions following engagement of some kind.

Figure 13.3: The Evaluator's Toolbox: Conversion rate

Conversion rate	Applications
An indicator of effectiveness and efficiency, the conversion rate is a ratio: the number of people who a took a desired action divided by the number of people contacted or involved or exposed (it can also be expressed as a percentage)	■ The numeric response to ads with call-to-action codes (i.e., how many persons exposed to the ad actually called the number?) ■ The number of people (or visits/hits) to a website who attended the event (or requested additional information, or registered) ■ The number of people travelling to a destination after requesting/receiving specific information or watching an ad ■ The ratio of visitors who bought something, or otherwise responded to a sponsor/exhibitor/supplier, to the total number of those exposed ■ The ratio of returnees (or planning to return) to the total number of attendees

Evaluation by attendees

Many meetings simply ask attendees for their feedback, including evaluation of speakers and venue, or whether or not they gained important knowledge or skills, but that is not really an ROI for the company or association that paid for the event. The problem in going beyond this feedback method is that of proving cause and effect, especially because a single meeting or event is unlikely to have long-term impacts. The Kirkpatrick model described in the previous chapter can be adapted as an approach to evaluating meeting outcomes.

In some cases it is enough to know that attendees were satisfied, leaving it to them to evaluate the benefits, but it is a rather superficial form of evaluation. Usually the evaluator will want to measure satisfaction levels in the context of other effectiveness measures, and importance-performance evaluation will be beneficial.

Research note

Severt, D., Wang, Y., Chen, P-J & Breiter, D. (2007). Examining the motivation, perceived performance, and behavioral intentions of convention attendees: Evidence from a regional conference. *Tourism Management, 28,* 399–408.

Abstract: This study assessed convention attendee motivations, performance evaluation, satisfaction, and behavioral intentions in a regional conference setting. Data was collected from conference attendees in the southeast United States. The findings revealed a five-dimension conference motivation: (1) activities and opportunities, (2) networking, (3) convenience of conference, (4) education benefits and (5) products and deals. Furthermore, the relationships between attendee's evaluation of conference performance, satisfaction judgment, and behavioral intention were examined. The relationships between educational activities, overall satisfaction, word-of-mouth, and intent to return were found to be significant. Recommendations to the meeting planners for conferences are provided based on the results.

Keywords: Motivation; Performance; Satisfaction; Behavioral intention; Convention

Figure 13.4: The Evaluator's Toolbox: Sample attendee evaluation form

Attendee evaluation	Technique
Satisfaction and Quality	Q: How satisfied are you with the following? OR Q: Rate the following attributes in terms of quality. A rating scale can be used with numeric values or words (e.g., 1 = poor, or completely unsatisfied and 5 = completely satisfied or excellent). A variation is to ask for the degree of agreement with statements such as: "I learned a great deal" (from completely disagree to completely agree)
Quality of Programme	▪ The speakers (name them?) ▪ Plenary sessions ▪ Proceedings or other documents provided ▪ The teachers/trainers/moderators ▪ The usefulness of information provided (or skills taught) ▪ What you learned ▪ Group sessions ▪ Social programme ▪ Networking that benefits you ▪ Information to take with you (or available to access in the future) ▪ The dates ▪ The length (overall, and daily)
Quality of Service	▪ Information available to you ▪ The registration process ▪ Registration fees ▪ Overall cost ▪ The venue overall ▪ The location ▪ Logistical arrangements (local travel, shuttles, tours) ▪ Hotel or other accommodation ▪ Food and beverages ▪ Entertainment ▪ Staff ▪ Volunteers
Overall Satisfaction	Q: Everything considered, how satisfied are you with the entire event experience? (use a numeric scale or words) OR Q: Did you get good value for your time and money invested? (use Yes/No, or a scale)
Additional topics	Q: What would you change? Recommendations for Improvement? (write in) Q: How did you lean about the event? What information source was most important? (provide options) Q: How likely are you to return to this event (next time)? (very unlikely to very likely)

13.2.2 Charity events (fund raisers)

The main goal is to raise money for worthwhile causes, but how much of it goes to administration or fees? That is both an ethical and efficiency question, as increasing the amount of money raised with lower input costs should be the primary long-term aim. O'Toole (2011:237) suggested that raising at least twice the cost of the event is a suitable minimum ROI. Other output KPIs might include raising awareness and networking.

Post-event fundraising might be enhanced by the event, but linking those two could be difficult, especially for established charities that are already in the fund-raising business. Many such events are instruments of social marketing, in which case the event helps in changing behaviour. Examples include anti-smoking or drinking, or changing attitudes towards segments of society.

Figure 13.5: Goals and KPIs for charity events

Recommended goals for charity events (fund raisers)	Sample KPIs
▪ Raise money (set targets) for charity/cause. ▪ Foster awareness of, and long-term support for (the event and a cause) ▪ Help change behaviour (to be specified, as in stop smoking)	▪ The ratio of money raised to direct expenditures plus admin costs ▪ Attachment to the cause fostered among participants and volunteers ▪ Awareness generated of the cause among target audiences ▪ Positive mass and social media coverage (tied to image, reputation and brand values)

13.2.3 Exhibitions

World's Fairs are a special category (often called 'expos') and are not considered here. The most common exhibitions are trade shows and consumer shows, and the special evaluation issues pertain to setting (does it work for the purposes of informing, marketing and sales?), motives and satisfactions of attendees and exhibitors, and impacts, including the specific benefits realized by owners and exhibitors.

CEIR, the *Centre for Exhibition Industry Research (www.ceir.org)* offers members a number of useful evaluation tools including an "exhibitor retention benchmarking tool, economic impact calculator, event performance analyzer and ROI toolkit". Some of their benchmarking metrics are net square footage (i.e., exhibit space), number of exhibitors, the number of professional attendees (these are likely the main target segment) and inflation-adjusted revenue from different sources.

ROI for exhibitors – the people and companies renting space at a show – can be expressed in sales, reach (the percentage of potential audience they contacted), networking among producers/suppliers, and the number of qualified leads obtained through engagement. Exhibitors are also very interested in knowing in advance what they will need, or how to optimize their floor space, number of staff, and means of attracting and engaging attendees. 'Engagement' is really the key, as having numerous attendees pass by an exhibit without stopping for information or to discuss the products and services on offer is a waste of time and money for the exhibitor. Increasingly the exhibition industry is focusing on experience and emotion to engage the consumer or professional buyer, as online marketing is a persistent threat.

Figure 13.6: Goals and KPIs for exhibitions

Recommended goals for exhibitions (trade and consumer shows)	Sample KPIs
Provide exhibitors with an optimum environment to achieve their marketing goals.	▪ Maximum exposure to the attendees (a matter of location and design) ▪ Maximum engagement with attendees (time spent, questions asked, information exchanged) ▪ Number of qualified leads generated ▪ Sales generated ▪ High exhibitor satisfaction and loyalty to the show
Meet the needs and exceed the expectations of attendees.	▪ High attendee satisfaction and loyalty ▪ High engagement, assessed through surveys and systematic observation of movement, time spent with exhibitors, overall length of visit ▪ High satisfaction

Research note

Breiter, D., & Millman, A. (2007). Predicting exhibitor levels of satisfaction in a large convention center. *Event Management,* **10**, 133–143.

The objectives of this research project were to identify tangible and intangible elements of service that exhibitors encounter while they participate in a tradeshow, to rank their relative importance, and to measure to what extent these service elements were delivered by a convention center. By understanding the importance/performance aspects of service from the customers' perspective, and the performance gaps, convention centers will be able to design and implement quality service assurance programmes to maintain a competitive edge in the marketplace. Additionally, this project sought to identify predictors of exhibitor satisfaction and intent to exhibit again at the facility.

Keywords: Exhibitor satisfaction; Service elements; Convention Center; Future intent

13.2.4 Corporate events

A broad category, this includes so-called experiential marketing, live communications and events tied to sponsorship, all usually within the corporate sphere. The influence of Pine and Gilmore (*The Experience Economy*, 1999) can be seen in the corporate world's latching on to events to connect with potential and existing customers in an emotional way that fosters brand loyalty, not just brand awareness.

According to Wood (2009b) who studied experiential marketing and events, there are three pertinent levels of evaluation: the event, consumer experiences, and consumer responses. A vast literature exists on what corporations want and how they do, or should go about evaluation and determining their ROI.

Research note

Wood, E. (2009b). Evaluating Event Marketing: Experience or Outcome? *Journal of Promotion Management*, **15**, 247–268.

The research presents a critical evaluation of the current methods used to measure the effectiveness of experiential marketing techniques. The article begins by reviewing the literature relating to event and experiential marketing and existing appropriate evaluation techniques.

One commercial approach called "sponsormap" has an application specifically for experiential marketing through events (www.sponsormap.com), with measures of effectiveness based on the five key stages of the "sponsormap" model:

"*Attention*: The point of initial exposure to the event by an audience while the audience is enjoying an event/property.

Understanding: The levels to which people are able to recall the brand of an event/property.

Engagement: The passion an audience has for the brand-owned event.

Appreciation: The gratitude or appreciation people may feel toward the brand as a result of the event experience.

Commitment: The change in attitudes or behavior that is a direct result of the experiential marketing activity."

Figure 13.7: Goals and KPIs for corporate events

Recommended goals for corporate events	Sample KPIs
▪ Engage customers with the experience in order to increase brand/service awareness, perceived quality, purchase and loyalty	▪ Heightened awareness of brand and brand values ▪ Change in attitudes about the brand or service from neutral or negative to positive ▪ Increase in intent, purchase and loyalty
▪ Manage the experience in order to maximize positive, enduring memories	▪ Zero negative critical incidents ▪ Increase in excellent service or exceptional experience from attendee's perspective ▪ Recall and word-of-mouth recommendations after the event

13.3 Festivals and cultural celebrations; the arts

By definition festivals are themed, public celebrations – although the name and variations like *'fest'* are often misused, especially for commercial purposes. If they are truly held for the public then there are issues of equity: can everyone afford to go? Is social exclusion a deliberate or unintentional effect?

'Communitas' (Turner, 2012) is a primary factor in celebration, that is bringing people together in a manner that fosters a sense of belonging and sharing among equals. Numerous community festivals exist for this purpose, aiming for little more than giving everyone a happy experience, but increasingly social inclusion, economic and community development goals are part of their purpose. The evaluator might start by first determining if a celebration is organic, springing from the community and a reflection of its character, or induced as a policy instrument.

Sometimes the theme is contentious, as when one group supports and another opposes the object of celebration, or the way in which it is celebrated. This issue particularly applies to heritage commemorations because historical events and people have symbolic meanings that are not shared by everyone. The goals of festivals are many and varied, some being for profit and others being produced or supported as part of public policy initiatives including. In the not-for-profit sector financial risks are high and failures common. The point is, evaluation will cover any and all of the purposes and uses related to events and tourism.

Figure 13.8: Festivals and cultural celebrations, key evaluation challenges

Festivals and cultural celebrations	Some key evaluation challenges
<ul><li>Festivals</li><li>Heritage commemorations</li><li>Carnivals; Mardi Gras</li><li>Religious rites</li><li>Pilgrimage</li><li>Parades</li></ul>	<ul><li>The roles of volunteers are often critical; how can volunteerism be valued and volunteers evaluated?</li><li>Evaluating co-created experiences (e.g., how to assess belonging and sharing)</li><li>Distinguishing between generic and event-specific benefits (i.e., between casual attendees and the highly involved)</li><li>Evaluating both resident and tourist interests</li><li>Defining and measuring perceptions of authenticity</li><li>Underlying values might conflict</li><li>How can the imputed social and cultural benefits of celebrations be proved? What evidence is acceptable?</li><li>Perceptions of crowding are important to satisfaction (some people prefer a crowd!)</li><li>Crowd behaviour is frequently a source of risk</li></ul>

Figure 13.9: Goals and KPIs for festivals and cultural celebrations

Recommended goals for festivals and cultural celebrations	Sample KPIs
▪ Preserve the authenticity of valued traditions	▪ Perceived authenticity by visitors, residents and other stakeholders as measured though surveys and interviews
▪ Maximise community engagement, sense of ownership and participation	▪ Increase voluntarism (number/commitment/retention) ▪ Increase civic pride ▪ Increase commitment to the event
▪ Aim for a consensus on the legitimacy of theme and programme	▪ Stakeholder engagement to achieve consensus

13.3.1 Special considerations for the Arts

Festivals often have an arts theme, and most encompass the arts in some form.

A usual classification of the arts includes visual, performing, literary and temporary – the latter including installations – and all of these can be presented as stand-alone special events. Intrinsic value is a dominant paradigm in the world of arts and culture, meaning that the use of quantitative metrics is often unwanted. Arts and cultural events are valued by many without reference to any extrinsic value such as ROI or economic impact. The use of Return on Objectives and participant evaluation is therefore often more applicable.

Figure 13.10: Arts and entertainment key evaluation challenges

Arts & entertainment	Some key evaluation challenges
▪ Scheduled Concerts, Shows, Theatre ▪ Art Exhibits Installations ▪ Temporary Art ▪ Award Ceremonies	▪ Applying both intrinsic and extrinsic measures of merit and worth, as many people view the arts as essential to culture and civilization ▪ Values and preferences vary greatly when it comes to arts and entertainment ▪ How to judge quality in the arts? (Quality of performances, and of events)

Williams and Bowdin (2007) examined the evaluation as practiced by seven UK arts festivals. The broad aims of these festivals included: educating the public; being accessible; reflecting or sustaining culture and traditions; fostering innovation and excellence; advancing arts appreciation; promoting citizen well-being in an holistic sense, and achieving/maintaining an international reputation. These arts-specific aims have to be balanced with financial realities, and in some cases growth was desired. Reasons for evaluating their events included both the desire to learn and improve and for accountability to funding agencies.

All seven festivals evaluated financial performance (e.g. box office receipts compared to sales/revenue targets; grants and sponsorship) and the following are other evaluation subjects identified by Williams and Bowdin, some of which are generic and some arts-specific.

- The relationships between artistic programming and audience are important, such as audience acceptance, satisfaction, and loyalty
- Marketing effectiveness (demand, catchment areas); public relations
- Judging artistic performance
- Artist satisfaction
- Educational effectiveness
- Staff performance

Audience research can include surveys for formal feedback on motivation, learning, satisfaction, loyalty, response to advertising and acceptance of innovation, while qualitative methods such as focus groups and observation of audience reactions can be useful. Media and social media analysis can provide important input. Feedback from sponsors and artistic promoters or agents will sometimes be essential. The relative values and costs/risks associated with programming elements might become an issue to evaluate, similar to portfolio asset valuation.

As documented by Derrett (2015:286) a variety of objectives are found in the culture and arts literature. These represent a mix of intrinsic and extrinsic values, leading to both quantitative and qualitative methods and measures: environmental enhancement, or culture-led development (of places); well-being or personal development; social capital; community building; cultural health and sustainability.

Artists and arts events have concerns not found in other festivals and events and might measure success in any of these terms:

- New performances (a measure of innovation or growth)
- Opportunities for generating income for artists, and revenue for events
- Interactions, such as among local and foreign artists
- Innovation and creativity in the art form being celebrated or featured
- Audience education and growth

Judging artistic quality

Perhaps the most difficult evaluation form to master (and occasionally to defend against accusations of bias or incompetence) is that of artistic quality. The perils of judging also apply to certain forms of athletic competition, such as ice skating. Three basic approaches are:

1 The recruitment of experienced experts, who presumably can tell good from bad, to rank performances (e.g. gold, silver, bronze).

2 Expert judges who are trained to evaluate performance against very specific technical and artistic quality criteria (such as the ability to perform certain techniques) resulting in a numeric score.

3 The use of the audience, consumers, or general public to vote.

The latter, sometimes referred to as the "peoples' choice" has become popular for television shows desiring mass audience participation, and is a feature of many wine or cooking competitions where taste is always highly variable.

Figure 13.11: Arts evaluation goals and KPIs

Recommended goals for arts evaluation	Sample KPIs
▪Employ the appropriate judging method for each performance.	▪No bias detected ▪High support from artists
▪Consult artists on all matters of evaluation	▪High satisfaction among artists
▪Educate audiences and the public about arts and artistic evaluation methods	▪Increased knowledge among audience and public
▪Foster arts participation and support in the community	▪Increased support for the arts

13.3.2 Special considerations for ethnic and multicultural celebrations

Special considerations apply when culture and tradition are featured. *Cultural appropriation* describes the unsanctioned and inappropriate use of symbols, artefacts or other aspects of one culture by another. *Authenticity* is usually important to attendees, especially cultural event tourists, but it has a number of connotations and requires attention to different stakeholder perspectives.

Multicultural festivals are intended to bring people together, foster sharing and understanding, and provide unique programming to the public. But the very nature of the collaboration required might produce tensions and disputes about goals, programming, interpretations and the division of costs and revenues. Evaluators will have to be extra-sensitive and employ some form of participatory evaluation to ensure that all voices are heard and satisfied in the process.

Figure 13.12: Goals and KPIs for ethnic and multicultural celebrations

Recommended goals for ethnic and multicultural celebrations	Sample KPIs
Maintain authenticity as defined by the cultural hosts/producers.	▪High acceptance of theme and programme (possibly aim for consensus) within the host community
Share authentic cultural experiences with guests in a manner that fosters education and respect for the hosts.	▪High levels of host and guest satisfaction ▪Increased positive visitor attitudes and learning as tested by pre-and post interviews or surveys
Maximise benefits for the hosts.	▪Use full cost/benefit evaluation, both for tangibles and intangibles

13.3.3 Special considerations for entertainment

There are numerous travelling shows that fit into this category, from the three-ring circus to Cirque du Soleil, musical theatre to concerts by pop music stars. The majority are in the private, for-profit domain. Packaging a bunch of shows can be called a festival. In the entertainment business promoters and the venues want to make a profit, artists want to sell music and gain exposure, host cities enjoy any tourism that is generated, and the public gains from having more choices and experiences. Two key measures are almost always up front: ticket sales and customer satisfaction, as both are crucial to the business. Concerts can be cancelled when advance sales fall short of expectations, and a disgruntled audience will ensure that bad publicity results. Problems with ticket sales have caused a lot of heartache and complaining about the entertainment business.

Injuries and deaths at rock concerts and other shows have led to a host of laws and regulations concerning safety. For specific news and advice see Crowdsafe. com. Additional concerns include sexual harassment, drug and alcohol abuse, waste (including hazardous materials) and noise pollution, all of which require special provisions and evaluation of effectiveness.

13.4 Sport events

The athlete is often the focus of attention, especially in elite sports. Overall, the athlete's experience will entail meeting specifications for accreditation, security, drugs and alcohol, sex, accompanying persons, transport, venue accessibility, housing, food, medical and psychological support, training, media relations and communications. MacIntosh and Dill (2015) reported on an evaluation of athletes' satisfaction, and cautioned about a number of special considerations including age differences, social inclusion versus discrimination, and in general the need for involving athletes in the planning and evaluation of events. They also drew attention to the particular needs of Paralympic athletes; the involvement of persons with disabilities poses certain challenges to evaluators, including the adequacy of provisions like medical support, accessibility and dealing with the media.

Figure 13.13: Sport events, key evaluation challenges

Sport events	Some key evaluation challenges
▪League play	▪Sports and sport venues generally must conform to strict specifications
▪Championships	▪Safety is often an issue owing to crowd dynamics
▪Participation events (amateur competitions)	▪Injury is always a concern for athletes
▪One-off meets and tours	▪Participation sport entails quite different motivations and benefits compared to spectator sports
▪Fun events	▪Can sports be fun without competition?
▪Sport festivals	▪Many people value sports intrinsically, believing they are important for health and developmental reasons
	▪The bidding process for sport events, especially the largest, entails high costs and many risks
	▪The costs of bidding and hosting major sport events has become prohibitive for many destinations – what are the options?
	▪It is easy to forecast tourism benefits and difficult to prove that benefits exceed costs

Benkendorff and Pearce (2012) summarized the literature on sport participation and spectatorship from a psychological perspective. Research on the motives of spectators is quite extensive, with a number of key theoretical concepts being especially applicable, namely role identity theory and leisure or ego involvement. Wann (1995) developed a sports fan motivation scale, Trail and James (2001) a sport consumption motivation scale, and Funk et al. (2001) a Sport Interest Inventory. Regarding participants, researchers have examined their levels of involvement and event travel careers (Getz and McConnell, 2011), with foundation theory provided by serious leisure (Stebbins, 2006), and social worlds (Unruh, 1980).

While the evaluation of service quality might be similar for most types of event, in sports the evaluation of participants and spectators must take into account a number of unique motives and expectations. The evaluator has to understand why people are attending or participating in order to know what questions to ask.

13.4.1 Special considerations for participation events

The participant is the focus, usually being amateur athletes but possibly a mix of professional and amateur. Organisers have numerous logistical challenges depending on the type of sport and its setting, and while many are part of a formal sport governing system with specifications, others are one-of-a kind and designed to offer something quite unique. Young et al. (2015) examined the benefits sought by participants in Masters Games, as these are typically older athletes, and in contrast, Kristiansen et al. (2015) examined the special case of parents and others accompanying youth to participate in sport events.

Figure 13.14: Goals and KPIs for participation sport events

Sample goals for participation sport events	Sample KPIs
Attract domestic and international participants	▪ Numbers and profiles of visitors ▪ Use involvement (both attitudes and behavioural measures) as a segmentation tool and a means to better understand motivation, benefits desired, expectations, loyalty versus novelty-seeking
Exceed the expectations of participants	▪ Visitor surveys measuring importance and performance, overall satisfaction, future intentions
Grow the reputation of the event	▪ Mass and social media monitoring to reveal positive and negative stories, misinformation, comparative image

Research note

Getz, D., & McConnell, A. (2014) Comparing trail runners and mountain bikers: Motivation, involvement, portfolios, and event-tourist careers. *Journal of Convention & Event Tourism*, **15** (1) 69-100.

Amateur trail runners and endurance mountain bikers are compared with regard to motivation, involvement in their sport, competitive-event portfolios, and event-travel careers. Participants in two destination events produced by a for-profit company constitute the sample frame, with the respondents having answered a sub-set of identical questions on an online, post-event evaluation survey. The two 'destination events' differ considerably in terms of the gender of participants, with a much higher proportion of females in the running event. Both samples were revealed to have a fairly high level of involvement in their sport, but a large proportion of participants in both events also participated in a wider portfolio of challenging sports.

13.4.2 Special considerations for spectator sports

Many spectators are also sport tourists who follow their team or sport to different cities and countries. What motivates and defines a fan? What experiences do they value? Are they high-yield event tourists?

Bodet (2015) examined the sport spectator, including the sub-category of 'fans' and argued for segmentation to reflect different motives and expectations of sport spectators. Wann and Branscombe (1993) developed a sport fan continuum that allows for multiple levels of attachment (to sport and teams), loyalty and identification. Funk and James (2001) advanced a psychological continuum model (PCM) that covers awareness, attraction, attachment and allegiance in relation to events, teams or the sport.

Figure 13.15: Goals and KPIs for spectator sport events

Recommended goals for spectator sport events	Sample KPIs
Provide a satisfying, memorable experience for all spectators	▪ High satisfaction levels ▪ Increasing loyalty (segment the audience in terms of motivation/benefits expected, identification with the sport, event and team, and participation in clubs or fan groups; track changes)
Provide a safe, comfortable experience for all spectators	▪ Reduced, or zero tolerance, of crime and rowdy behaviour ▪ Reduced or zero incidence of misbehaviour attributable to substance abuse

Study questions

1 Discuss appropriate and feasible methods for obtaining attendee, participant, and external-stakeholder feedback on a convention, exhibition, festival and sport event.

2 How can the evaluator of an arts festival or concert draw conclusions about authenticity and quality?

3 Compare and contrast the motivations and needs of sport spectators and participants, then discuss the implications for evaluators.

Recommended additional readings and sources

Crowdsafe.com

SponsorMap (www.sponsormap.com),

References

Alkin, M. and Christie, C. (2004). An evaluation theory tree, In: M. Alkin, (ed), *Evaluation Roots: Tracing Theorists' Views and Influences,* pp. 12-65. California: Sage.

Allen, J., O'Toole, W., Harris, R. and McDonnell, I. (2011*). Festival and Special Event Management,* 5th ed. Brisbane: Wiley Australia.

Alonso, A. (2016). Stakeholders, collaboration, food and wine: The case of Jumilla's Gastronomic Days. *Journal of Convention and Event Tourism,* **17** (3), 173-191.

American Evaluation Association (AEA) (http://www.eval.org) -The Principles (http://www.eval.org/p/cm/ld/fid=51)

Anderson, D. (2017). Intent scales in economic impact studies: A case study. *Event Management, 21,*101–108.

Andersson, T., Armbrecht, J. and Lundberg, E. (2012): Estimating use and non-use values of a music festival. *Scandinavian Journal of Hospitality and Tourism, 12* (3), 215-231

Andersson, T., Armbrecht, J. and Lundberg, E. (2016) Triple impact assessments of the 2013 European athletics indoor championship in Gothenburg. *Scandinavian Journal of Hospitality and Tourism,* **16** (2), 158-179.

Andersson, T., Armbrecht, J. and Lundberg, E. (2017). The use and non-use value of events: A conceptual framework. In: Lundberg, E., Armbrecht, J., Andersson, T. and Getz, D. (Eds.), *The Value of Events,* pp. 89-104. London: Routledge.

Andersson, T. and Getz, D. (2008). Stakeholder management strategies of festivals. *Journal of Convention and Event Tourism,* **9** (3), 199-220.

Andersson, T., Getz, D. and Mykletun, R. (2013). Sustainable festival populations: an application of organisational ecology. *Tourism Analysis,* **18** (6), 621-634.

Andersson, T., Getz, D., Vujicic, S., Robinson, R. and Cavicchi, A. (2016). Preferred travel experiences of foodies: An application of photo elicitation. *Journal of Vacation Marketing,* **22** (1), 55-67.

Andersson, T., Jutbring, H. and Lundberg, E. (2013).When a music festival goes veggie: Communication and environmental impacts of an innovative food strategy. *International Journal of Event and Festival Management,* **4** (3), 224-235.

Andersson, T. and Lundberg, E. (2013). Commensurability and sustainability: Triple impact assessment of a tourism event. *Tourism Management, 27,* 1-11.

APEX Event Specifications Guide Template (www.conventionindustry.org).

Arcodia, C. (2002). The role of simulation gaming in event management education. *Journal of Convention and Exhibition Management,* **4** (1),19-28.

Barron, P. and Rihova, I. (2011). Motivation to volunteer: A case study of the Edinburgh International Magic Festival. *International Journal of Event and Festival Management,* **2** (3), 202-217.

Basu, R. and Wright, J. (2003). *Quality Beyond Six Sigma.* London: Elsevier.

Baum, T. (2006). *Human Resource Management for Tourism, Hospitality and Leisure: An International perspective*. Thomson Learning.

Baum, T., Deery, M., Hanlon, C., Lockstone, L. and Smith, K. (eds.) (2009). *People and Work in Events and Conventions: A Research Perspective*. Oxford: CABI

Beard, C. and Russ, W. (2017). Event evaluation and design: Human experience mapping. *Event Management*, **21**, 365-374.

Benkendorff, P. and Pearce, P. (2012). The psychology of events. In: Page, S. and Connell, J. (eds.), *The Routledge Handbook of Events*, pp.165-185. London: Routledge.

Biaett, V. and Hultsman, W. (2015). Everybody loves a parade . . . but how many is everybody? *Event Management*, **19**, 151-157.

Berridge, G. (2007). *Events Design and Experience*. Amsterdam: Elsevier.

Berridge, G. (2014). The Gran Fondo and sportive experience: An exploratory look at cyclists' experiences and professional event staging. *Event Management*, **18**, 75-88.

Better Evaluation (http://www.betterevaluation.org)

Bodet, G. (2015). The spectators' perspective. In: Parent, M. and Chappelet, J-L. (2015). *Routledge Handbook of Sports Event Management*, pp. 153-180. Abingdon, Oxon: Routledge.

Breiter, D. and Millman, A. (2007). Predicting exhibitor levels of satisfaction in a large convention center. *Event Management*, **10**, 133–143.

Brown, S., Getz, D., Pettersson, R. and Wallstam, M. (2015). Event evaluation: Definitions, concepts and a state of the art review. *International Journal of Event and Festival Management*, **6** (2), 135-157.

Brown, S. and Hutton, A. (2013). Developments in the real-time evaluation of audience behaviour at planned events. *International Journal of Event and Festival Management*, **4** (1), 43-55.

Business Dictionary
www.businessdictionary.com/definition/key-performance-indicators-KPI.html
www.businessdictionary.com/definition/ organisational-culture.html

Carlsen, J., Getz, D. and Soutar, G. (2000). Event evaluation research. *Event Management*, **6** (4), 247-257.

CEIR, the Centre for Exhibition Industry Research (www.ceir.org)

Chalip, L. (2006). Towards social leverage of sport events. *Journal of Sport and Tourism*, **11** (2), 109-127.

Christie, C. and Alkin, M. (2008). Evaluation theory tree re-examined. *Studies in Educational Evaluation*, **34** (3), 131-135.

Clark, T. and Salaman, G. (1998). Telling tales: Management gurus' narratives and the construction of managerial identity. *Journal of Management Studies*, *35* (2), 137-161.

Clifton, N., O'Sullivan, D. and Pickernell, D. (2012). Capacity building and the contribution of public festivals: Evaluating "Cardiff 2005". *Event Management*, **16** (1), 77-91.

Coghlan, A., Preskill, H. and Catsambas, T. (2003). An Overview of Appreciative Inquiry in Evaluation. *New Directions for Evaluation*, **2003** (100), 5-22.

Collins, A. and Cooper, C. (2017). Measuring and managing the environmental impact of festivals: The contribution of the ecological footprint. *Journal of Sustainable Tourism*, **25** (1), 148-162.

Convention Industry Council: APEX Event Specifications Guide Template (www. conventionindustry.org).

Crespi-Vallbona, M. and Richards, G. (2007). The meaning of cultural festivals: Stakeholder perspectives in Catalunya. *International Journal of Cultural Policy*, **13** (1), 103-122.

CrowdSafe (Crowdsafe.com)

Davies, K., Ritchie, C. and Jaimangal-Jones, D. (2015). A multi-stakeholder approach: Using visual methodologies for the investigation of intercultural exchange at cultural events. *Journal of Policy Research in Tourism, Leisure and Events*, **7** (2), 150-172.

De Geus, S., Richards, G. and Toepoel, V. (2016). Conceptualisation and operationalisation of event and festival experiences: Creation of an event experience scale. *Scandinavian Journal of Hospitality and Tourism*, **16** (3), 274-296.

Derrett, R. (2015). *The Complete Guide to Creating Enduring Festivals*. New York: Wiley.

Drucker, P. (1954). *The Practice of Management*. New York: Harper and Brothers.

Dwyer, L., Forsyth, P. and Dwyer, W. (2010). *Tourism Economics and Policy*. Bristol: Channel View.

Dwyer, L. and Forsyth, P. (2017). Event evaluation: Approaches and new challenges. In: Lundberg, E., Armbrecht, J., Andersson, T. and Getz, D. (Eds.). *The Value of Events*, 105-123. London: Routledge.

EMBOK: Event Management Body of Knowledge (http://www.embok.org/index. php/embok-model)

Evaluation Wiki (EvaluationWiki.org).

Evaluation Center, Western Michigan University (https://wmich.edu/evaluation); (https://wmich.edu/evaluation/checklists)

EventImpacts (www.eventimpacts.com).

Experience Institute (2017). Decision to Attend Study for Conventions and Exhibitions (https://www.iaee.com/resources/decision-to-attend-study/).

Fetterman, D., Rodriguez, L., Wandersman, A. and O'Sullivan, R. (2015). Collaborative, participatory and empowerment evaluation: Building a stronger conceptual foundation for stakeholder involvement approaches to evaluation. *American Journal of Evaluation*, **35** (1), 144-148.

Fotiadis, A. and Sigala, M. (2015). Developing a framework for designing an events management training simulation (EMTS). *Journal of Hospitality, Leisure, Sport and Tourism Education*, **16**, 59-71.

Fox, K., Humberstone, B. and Dubnewick, M. (2014). Cycling into sensoria: Embodiment, leisure and tourism. *Tourism Review International*, **18**, 71-85.

Funk, D. and James, J. (2001). The psychological continuum model: A conceptual framework for understanding an individual's psychological connection to sport. *Sport Management Review*, **4** (2), 119-150.

Funk, D., Mahony, D., Nakazawa, M. and Hirakawa, S. (2001). Development of the sport interest inventory (SII): Implications for measuring unique consumer motives at team sporting events. *International Journal of Sports Marketing and Sponsorship*, **3** (3), 38-63.

Getz, D. (2005). *Event Management and Event Tourism* (2d ed.). New York: Cognizant.

Getz, D. (2007). *Event Studies: Theory, Research and Policy for Planned Events*. Oxford: Butterworth-Heinemann.

Getz, D. (2009). Policy for sustainable and responsible festivals and events: Institutionalization of a new paradigm. *Journal of Policy Research in Tourism, Leisure and Events*, **1** (1), 61-78.

Getz, D. (2012). *Event Studies: Theory, Research and Policy for Planned Events* (2d ed.). Oxford: Routledge.

Getz, D. (2013). *Event Tourism: Concepts, International Case Studies and Research*. New York: Cognizant.

Getz, D. (2017). Developing a framework for sustainable event cities. *Event Management*, **21** (5), 575-591.

Getz, D. and Andersson, T. (2008). Sustainable festivals: On becoming an institution. *Event Management*, **12** (1), 1-17.

Getz, D., Andersson, T. and Larson, M. (2007). Festival stakeholder roles: Concepts and case studies. *Event Management*, **10** (2), 103-122.

Getz, D., Andersson, T., Robinson, R. and Vujicic, S. (2014). *Foodies and Food Tourism*. Bristol: Goodfellow.

Getz, D. and McConnell, A. (2011). Serious sport tourism and event travel careers. *Journal of Sport Management*, **25** (4), 326-338.

Getz, D. and McConnell, A. (2014). Comparing trail runners and mountain bikers: Motivation, involvement, portfolios and event-tourist careers. *Journal of Convention and Event Tourism*, **15** (1), 69-100.

Getz, D., O'Neill, M. and Carlsen, J. (2001). Service quality evaluation at events through service mapping. *Journal of Travel Research*, **39** (4) 380-390.

Getz, D. and Page, S. (2016). *Event Studies: Theory, Research and Policy for Planned Events*, 3d. ed. London: Routledge.

Getz, D. and Patterson, I. (2013). Social worlds as a framework for examining event and travel careers. *Tourism Analysis*, **18** (5), 485-501.

Getz, D., Svensson, B., Pettersson, R. and Gunnervall, A. (2012). Hallmark events: Definition, goals and planning process. *International Journal of Event Management Research* **7** (1/2), 47-67.

Global Reporting Initiative Sustainability Reporting Guidelines and Event Organizers Sector Supplement. (https://www.globalreporting.org/resourcelibrary/EOSS-G3.1-Complete.pdf)

Goldblatt, J. (2011). *Special Events*, 6th ed. New York: Wiley.

Goolaup, S. and Mossberg, L. (2017). Exploring consumers' value co-creation in a festival context using a socio-cultural lens. In: Lundberg, E., Armbrecht, J., Andersson, T. and Getz, D. (Eds.), *The Value of Events*, pp.39-57. London: Routledge.

Green, B. (2001). Leveraging subculture and identity to promote sport events. *Sport Management Review*, **4** (1), 1-19.

Green, C. and Jones, I. (2005). Serious leisure, social identity and sport tourism. *Sport in Society*, **8** (2), 198-217.

Hall, M. (1994). Mega-events and their legacies. In: P. Murphy (Ed.), *Quality Management in Urban Tourism: Balancing Business and Environment*, pp, 109-123. University of Victoria.

Hall, M. (2012). Sustainable mega-events: Beyond the myth of balanced approaches to mega-event sustainability. *Event Management,* **16** (2), 119-131.

Hanlon, C. and Jago, L. (2012). Staffing for successful events. In: S. Page and J. Connell (Eds.), *The Routledge Handbook of Events,* pp. 304-315. Abingdon, UK: Routledge.

Harris, R. (2014). The role of large-scale sporting events in host community education for sustainable development: An exploratory case study of the Sydney 2000 Olympic Games. *Event Management,* **18** (3), 207-230.

Higham, J. and Hinch, T. (2009). *Sport and Tourism: Globalization, Mobility and Identity.* Oxford: Elsevier Butterworth Heinemann.

Holloway, I. and Wheeler, S. (2010). *Qualitative Research in Nursing and Healthcare,* 3rd. ed., Oxford: Wiley-Blackwell.

Institute on Governance (http://iog.ca/defining-governance/)

International Standards Organization (ISO). The Event Sustainability Management System. (http://www.iso20121.org/)

Iso-Ahola, S. E. (1980). *The Social Psychology of Leisure and Recreation.* Dubuque: Brown.

Jenkins, R. (1996). *Social Identity.* London: Routledge.

Jones, M. (2017). *Sustainable Event Management: A Practical Guide,* 2nd ed. London: Earthscan.

Jones, P. (2011). *Strategy Mapping for Learning Organizations.* Gower.

Kapferer, J. (1987). *Strategic Brand Management.* London: Kogan Page.

Kaplan, R. and Norton, D. (1992). The balanced scorecard – Measures that drive performance. *Harvard Business Review* (January–February), 71–79.

Kaplanidou, K., Jordan, J., Funk, L. and Ridinger, L. (2012). Recurring sport events and destination image perceptions: Impact on active sport tourist behavioral intentions and place attachment. *Journal of Sport Management,* **26,** 237-248.

Katsoni, V. and Vrondou, O. (2017) Marketing to occasional sporting event tourists: Profiles, travelling patterns and information channels. *Journal of Policy Research in Tourism, Leisure and Events,* **9** (2), 152-168.

Kellaghan, T. and Stufflebeam, D. (Eds.)(2003). *International Handbook of Educational Evaluation.* Dordrecht Netherlands: Springer.

King, K. (2012). Encouraging active identities and lifestyles, in R. Shipway and A. Fyall (Eds.) *International Sports Events: Impacts, Experiences and Identities,* 181-194. London: Routledge.

Kirkpatrick, D. and Kirkpatrick, J. (2007). *Implementing the Four Levels.* Berrett-Koehler Publishers.

Kirkup, N. (2012). Olympic tourists: Seeking a sense of belonging and the construction of social identities, in R. Shipway and A. Fyall (Eds.) *International Sports Events: Impacts, Experiences and Identities,* 169-180. London: Routledge.

Kristiansen, E., Roberts, G. and Lemyre, P-N. (2015). The sport parents' and entourage's perspective. In: Parent, M. and Chappelet, J-L. (2015). *Routledge Handbook of Sports Event Management,* pp. 183-202. Abingdon, Oxon: Routledge.

Laing, J. and Frost, W. (2010). How green was my festival: Exploring challenges and opportunities associated with staging green events. *International Journal of Hospitality Management,* **29** (2), 261-267.

Lamont, M. (2014). Authentication in sports tourism. *Annals of Tourism Research*, **45**, 1-17.

Lamont, M. and McKay, J. (2012). Intimations of postmodernity in sports tourism at the Tour de France. *Journal of Sport and Tourism*, **17** (4), 313-331.

Larson, M. (2009). Joint event production in the jungle, the park and the garden: Metaphors of event networks. *Tourism Management*, **30** (3), 393-399.

Lask, T. (2011). Cognitive maps: A sustainable tool for impact evaluation. *Journal of Policy Research in Tourism, Leisure and Events* **3** (1), 44-62.

Le Compte, M., Preissle, J. and Tesch, R. (1993). *Ethnography and Qualitative Design in Educational Research*, 2nd ed, Chicago: Academic Press.

Lee, I., King, K., Brown, G. and Shipway, R. (2014, July). *The nature of sport event space for social identity formation*. Paper presented at Global Events Congress VI, 9-11 July 2014, Adelaide, Australia.

Leopkey, B. and Parent, M. (2009). Risk management strategies by stakeholders in Canadian major sporting events. *Event Management*, **13** (3), 153–170.

Levy, S. (2010). The hospitality of the host: A cross-cultural examination of managerially facilitated consumer-to-consumer interactions. *International Journal of Hospitality Management*, **29** (2), 319-327.

Lundberg, E., Armbrecht, J., Andersson, T. and Getz, D. (Eds.) (2017). *The Value of Events*. London: Routledge.

McCabe, V., Poole, B., Weeks, P. and Leiper, N. (2000), *The Business and Management of Conventions*. John Wiley and Sons, Milton, Qld

McCarthy, K., Ondaatje, E., Laura, Z. and Brooks, A. (2004). *Gifts of the Muse: Reframing the Debate About the Benefits of the Arts*. Santa Monica, CA: Rand.

Mackay, K. and Crompton, J. (1988). A conceptual model of consumer evaluation of recreation service quality. *Leisure Studies*, **7** (1), 40-49.

MacIntosh, E. and Dill, S. (2015). The athletes' perspective. In: Parent, M. and Chappelet, J-L. (2015). *Routledge Handbook of Sports Event Management*, pp. 125-138. Abingdon, Oxon: Routledge.

Mackellar, J. (2014). *Event Audiences and Expectations*. Abingdon, Oxon: Routledge.

Malinowski, B. (1922). *Argonauts of the Western Pacific: An account of Native Enterprise and Adventure in the Archipelagoes of Melanesian New Guinea*. New York: Dutton.

Mead, M. (1935). *Sex and Temperament in Three Primitive Societies*. New York: Harper Collins.

Michelini, L., Iasevoli, G. and Theodoraki, E. (2017). Event venue satisfaction and its impact on sponsorship outcomes. *Event Management*, **21**, 319-331.

Miller, A. (2012). Understanding the 'event experience' of active sports tourists: Long distance endurance triathletes, in R. Shipway and A. Fyall (Eds.) *International Sports Events: Impacts, Experiences and Identities*, 99-112. London: Routledge.

Morgan, M. (2007). 'We're not the Barmy Army!': Reflections on the sports tourist experience. *International Journal of Tourism Research*, **9**, 361-372.

Morgan, M (2008). What makes a good festival? Understanding the event experience.*Event Management*, **12** (2), 81-93.

Morrison, A. (1995). *Hospitality and Travel Marketing*, 2d. ed. Albany, N.Y.: Delmar.

Mortazavi, R. and Heldt, T. (2017). Economic valuation of events: Combining methods based on revealed, stated and subjective preference data. In: Lundberg, E., Armbrecht, J., Andersson, T. and Getz, D. (Eds), *The Value of Events*, pp.124-135. London: Routledge.

Mossberg, L. and Getz, D. (2006). Stakeholder influences on the ownership and anagement of festival brands. *Scandinavian Journal of Hospitality and Tourism,* **6** (4), 308-326.

MPI - Meeting Professionals International. Meeting and Business Event Competency Standards (MBECS). (https://www.mpiweb.org/docs/...and.../ MBECS-Guide-APP-2-Standards.pdf)

O'Sullivan, D., Pickernell, D. and Senyard, J. (2009). Public sector evaluation of festivals and special events. *Journal of Policy Research in Tourism, Leisure and Events,* **1** (1), 19-36.

O'Toole, W. (2011). *Events Feasibility and Development: From Strategy to Operations.* Amsterdam: Butterworth-Heinemann.

O'Toole, W. and Mikolaitis, P. (2002). *Corporate Event Project Management.* N.Y: Wiley.

Palmer, C. (2005). An ethnography of Englishness: Experiencing identity through Tourism. *Annals of Tourism Research, 32* (1), 7-27.

Palmer, C. (2010). 'We close towns for a living': Spatial transformation and the Tour de France. *Social and Cultural Geography, 11* (8), 865-881.

Palmer, R. and Richards, G. (2010). *Eventful Cities: Cultural Management and Urban Revitalization.* Oxford: Butterworth-Heinemann.

Parasuraman, A., Zeithaml, V. and Berry, L. (1985). A conceptual model of service quality and its implications for future research. *Journal of Marketing,* **49**, 41-50.

Parasuraman, A., Zeithaml, V. and Berry, L. (1988). SERVQUAL: A multiple-item scale for measuring consumer perceptions of service quality. *Journal of Retailing,* **64** (1), 12-40.

Parent, M. and Seguin, B. (2007). Factors that led to the drowning of a world championship organising committee: A stakeholder approach. *European Sport Management Quarterly, 7* (2), 187–212.

Park, M., Daniels, M. J., Brayley, R. and Harmon, L. K. (2010). An analysis of service provision and visitor impacts using participant observation and photographic documentation: The National Cherry Blossom Festival. *Event Management,* **14** (2), 167-182.

Patton, M. (2008). *Utilization-Focused Evaluation,* 4th.ed. Thousand Oaks, CA: Sage.

Pawson, R. and Tilley, N (1997) *Realistic Evaluation,* London: Sage.

Pearce, P. and Zare, S. (2017). The orchestra model as the basis for teaching tourism experience design. *Journal of Hospitality and Tourism Management 30,* 55-64.

Peperkamp, E., Rooijackers, M. and Remmers, G-J. (2015). Evaluating and designing for experiential value: The use of visitor journeys. *Journal of Policy Research in Tourism, Leisure and Events, 7* (2),134-149.

Performance Appraisal (http://www.performance-appraisal.com/ratings.htm).

Pettersson, R. and Getz, D. (2009). Event experiences in time and space: A study of visitors to the 2007 World Alpine Ski Championships in Åre, Sweden. *Scandinavian Journal of Hospitality and Tourism, 9* (2-3), 308-326.

Pine, J. and Gilmore, J. (1999). *The Experience Economy.* Boston: Harvard Business School Press.

Potter, C. (2006). Program evaluation. In: M. Terre Blanche, K. Durrheim and D. Painter (Eds.), *Research in Practice: Applied Methods for the Social Sciences,* 2nd ed., pp. 410-428. Cape Town: UCT Press.

Pugh, C. and Wood, E. (2004). The strategic use of events within local government: A study of London Borough Councils. *Event Management,* **9** (1), 61–71.

Prebensen, N. (2010). Value creation through stakeholder participation: A case study of an event in the high north. *Event Management,* **14** (1), 37-52.

Prebensen, N. (2017). Successful event-destination collaboration through superior experience value for visitors. In: Lundberg, E., Armbrecht, J., Andersson, T. and Getz, D. (Eds.)(2017), *The Value of Events,* pp. 58-72. London: Routledge.

Preuss, H. (2007). The conceptualisation and measurement of mega sport event legacies. *Journal of Sport and Tourism,* **12** (3/4), 207-228.

Quinn, B. (2010). The European Capital Culture initiative and cultural legacy: An analysis of the cultural sector in the aftermath of Cork 2005. *Event Management,* **13** (4), 249-264.

Ramchandani, G., Coleman, R., , L., Shibli, S and Bingham. J. (2017). Valuing the inspirational impacts of major sports events. In: Lundberg, E., Armbrecht, J., Andersson, T. and Getz, D. (Eds.), *The Value of Events,* pp. 136-158. London: Routledge.

Richards, G. and Columbo, A. (2017). Creating network value: The Barcelona Sonar Festival as a global events hub. In: Lundberg, E., Armbrecht, J., Andersson, T. and Getz, D. (Eds.)(2017), *The Value of Events,* pp. 73-86. London: Routledge.

Rickly-Boyd, J. (2012). Lifestyle climbing: Toward existential authenticity. *Journal of Sport and Tourism,* **17** (2), 85-104.

Ritchie, J. R. B. (2000). Turning 16 days into 16 years through Olympic legacies. *Event Management,* **6** (2), 155-165.

Robertson, M., Rogers, P. and Leask, A. (2009). Progressing socio-cultural impact evaluation for festivals. *Journal of Policy Research in Tourism, Leisure and Events,* **1** (2), 156-169.

Rossi, P., Freeman, H. and Lipsey, M. (2004) *Evaluation. A Systematic Approach,* 7th ed. Thousand Oaks, CA: Sage.

Rossman, J. (2003). *Recreation Programming: Designing Leisure Experiences.* Urbana, IL: Sagamore.

Sadd, D. (2010). What is event-led regeneration? Are we confusing terminology or will London 2012 be the first games to truly benefit the existing population? *Event Management,* **13** (4), 265-275.

Schlenker, K., Edwards, D. and Wearing, S. (2012). Volunteering and events. In: S. Page and J. Connell (Eds.), *The Routledge Handbook of Events,* pp. 315- 325. Abingdon, UK: Routledge.

Scriven, M. (1991a). *Evaluation Thesaurus.* Newbury Park, CA: SAGE.

Scriven, M. (1991b). Prose and cons about goal-free evaluation. *American Journal of Evaluation,* **12**, (1), 55-63.

Scriven, M. (2007). *The Logic and Methodology of Checklists.* Western Michigan University. http://www.wmich.edu/evalctr/archive_checklists/papers/logicandmethodology_dec07.pdf

Senge, P. (1990). *The Fifth Discipline: The Art and Practice of The Learning Organization.* N.Y. Doubleday.

Shaw, C. (2005). *Revolutionize Your Customer Experience.* Basingstoke: Palgrave Macmillan.

Shaw, I., Greene, J. and Mark, M. (2006). *The Sage Handbook of Evaluation.* London: Sage.

Shipway, R. and Jones, I. (2007). Running away from home: Understanding visitor experiences and behaviour at sport tourism events. *International Journal of Tourism Research,* **9** (5), 373-383.

Shipway, R. and Jones, I. (2008). The great suburban Everest: An 'insiders' perspective on experiences at the 2007 Flora London Marathon. *Journal of Sport and Tourism,* **13** (1), 61-77.

Shipway, R., Holloway, I. and Jones, I. (2013). Organisations, practices, actors and events: Exploring inside the distance running social world. *International Review for the Sociology of Sport,* **48** (3), 259-276.

Shipway, R., King, K., Lee, S. and Brown, G. (2016). Understanding cycle tourism experiences at the Tour Down Under. *Journal of Sport and Tourism,* **20**, 21-39.

Silvers, J. (2008). *Risk Management for Meetings and Events.* Amsterdam: Butterworth-Heinemann.

Silvers, J., Bowdin, G., O'Toole, W. and Nelson, K. (2005). Towards an international event management body of knowledge (EMBOK). *Event Management,* **9**, 185-198.

Social Research Methods (*socialresearchmethods.net*) Evaluation Research.

Sponsormap (www.sponsormap.com)

Spradley, J. (1980) *Participant Observation.* N.Y.: Holt, Rinehart and Winston.

Stadler, R. and Jepson, A. (2017). Understanding the value of events for families and the impact upon their quality of life. In: Lundberg, E., Armbrecht, J., Andersson, T. and Getz, D. (Eds.), *The Value of Events,* pp. 159-177. London: Routledge.

Stebbins, R. (2006). *Serious Leisure: A Perspective for Our Time.* Somerset, NJ: Aldine Transaction Publications.

Stufflebeam, D. and Coryn, C. (2014). *Evaluation Theory, Models and Applications,* 2d. ed. San Francisco, CA: Jossey-Bass.

Sustainable Measures (http://www.sustainablemeasures.com/home)

Tarlow, P. (2002). *Event Risk Management and Safety.* N.Y.: Wiley

Thomas, R. and Wood, E. (2003). Event based tourism: A survey of local authority strategies in the UK. *Local Governance,* **29** (2), 127–136.

Trail, G. and James, J. (2001) The motivation scale for sport consumption: Assessment of the scale's psychometric properties. *Journal of Sport Behavior,* **24** (1), 108-127.

Tum, J., Norton, P. and Wright, J. (2006). *Management of Event Operations.* Amsterdam: Butterworth-Heinemann.

Turner, V. (1973). The center out there: Pilgrim's goal. *History of Religions,* **12** (3), 191-230.

Turner, E. (2012). *Communitas: The Anthropology of Collective Joy.* N.Y.: Palgrave Macmillan.

Tyrrell, B. and Ismail, J. (2005). A methodology for estimating the attendance and economic impact of an open-gate festival. *Event Management,* **9** (3), 111-118.

UK Department for Communities and Local Government Publications (2007). *Fire Safety Risk Assessment.*

Unruh, D. (1980). The nature of social worlds. *Pacific Sociological Review,* **23** (3), 271–296.

Urry, J. (2002). *The Tourist Gaze.* London: Sage.

Van Der Wagen, L. (2007). *Human Resource Management for Events.* Amsterdam: Butterworth-Heinemann.

Wann, D. (1995). Preliminary validation of the sport fan motivation scale. *Journal of Sport and Social Issues,* **19** (4), 377-396.

Wann, D. and Branscombe, N. (1993). Sports fans: Measuring degree of identification with their team. *International Journal of Sport Psychology,* **24** (1), 1-17.

Wann, D., Melnick, M., Russell, G. and Pease, D. (2001). *Sport fans: The psychology and social impact of spectators.* New York: Routledge.

Weed, M. and Bull, C. (2004). *Sports Tourism: Participants, Policy and Providers.* Oxford: Elsevier.

Weiss, O. (2001). Identity reinforcement in sport: Revisiting the symbolic interactionist legacy. *International Review for the Sociology of Sport,* **36** (4), 393-405.

What-When-How.com (http://what-when-how.com/social-sciences/methodology -social-science/)

Wikipedia

   https://en.wikipedia.org/wiki/SERVQUAL

   https://en.wikipedia.org/wiki/Triple_bottom_line

Williams, M. and Bowdin, G. (2007). Festival evaluation: An exploration of seven UK arts festivals. *Managing Leisure,* **12** (2), 187-203.

Williams, P., Gill, A. and Ponsford, I. (2007). Corporate social responsibility at tourism destinations: Toward a social license to operate. *Tourism Review International,* **11** (2), 133-144.

Wood, E. (2006) Measuring the social impacts of local authority events: a pilot study for a civic pride scale. *International Journal of Nonprofit and Voluntary Sector Marketing,* **11**, 165–179.

Wood, E. (2009a). An impact evaluation framework: Local government community festivals. *Event Management,* **12** (3/4), 171-185.

Wood, E. (2009b). Evaluating Event Marketing: Experience or Outcome? *Journal of Promotion Management,* **15**, 247–268.

Wood, E. (2017). The value of events and festivals in the age of austerity. In: Lundberg, E., Armbrecht, J., Andersson, T. and Getz, D. (Eds.), *The Value of Events,* pp. 10-35. London: Routledge.

Young, B., Bennett, A. and Seguin, B. (2015). Masters sport perspectives. In: Parent, M. and Chappelet, J-L. *Routledge Handbook of Sports Event Management,* pp. 139-162. Abingdon, Oxon: Routledge.

Ziakas, V. (2013). *Event Portfolio Planning and Management : A Holistic Approach.* Oxford: Routledge.

Index